Prokofiev: His Life and Times

Prokofiev

Natalia Savkina
Translated by Catherine Young

ISBN 0-86622-021-6

PAGANINIANA PUBLICATIONS, INC.
211 West Sylvania Avenue, Neptune City, New Jersey 07753

Contents

Prokofiev.

Introduction

Portrait of Prokofiev by Milkin (1932).

On the borderline of the 19th and the 20th centuries, Russia was living in expectation of tremendous social upheavals. "A whirlpool of growing sociopolitical complications" (Lenin), a critical exacerbation of all contradictions, the complexity of the spiritual and moral issues the country was facing could not fail to leave their mark on the Russian art of that time. It was distinguished by intense quests for new genres, new means of expression, new forms in which new contents could be embodied. In turn-of-the-century art, there was a striking abundance of trends, of diverse individualities and mutually exclusive directions, or, as Friedrich Engels astutely remarked, "most unbelievable and bizarre combinations of ideas springing up."

Like any other complex epoch of battles of minds, tastes, and schools, the turn of the century was marked by a great number of artistic discoveries. It was in those years that one of the most sparkling talents of Russian and world culture was formed: Sergei Prokofiev was making his first steps in art.

"He is a young, robust child of nature, a mustang who has been grazing in the wild," Moscow critic Yuli Engel exclaimed in delight and amazement, having heard the young musician perform for the first time. Prokofiev's fiery temperament was, as it turned out, extraordinarily attuned to his times. His music was enthusiastically received by many young composers and music critics with their eagerness to welcome the new, with their hatred of philistinism and "fineries," of senseless routine and cliches, of meaningless sound-making. It was also held in high regard by the most progressive leaders of Russian culture—Gorky, Lunacharsky, Mayakovsky, and others.

And yet, his innovative music did not at first easily find its way to the audiences. Prokofiev's immediate predecessors—composers of an older generation—did not at once see in their pupil an heir to the best traditions of the national culture. Prokofiev bewildered the strict faculties of conservatories, the straightlaced public of elegant, aristocratic St. Petersburg suburbia, the American audiences, and the enlightened artistic elite of Paris. Prokofiev's life was the thorny path of an artist who was great and unique in his errors, in the contradictions of a complicated human soul, as well as in his insights of genius.

From the very beginning, Prokofiev rejected the world many of his contemporaries recreated in their works—a world of chaos and destruction, dominated by moods of somber anxiety. To motives of human despair and isolation, Prokofiev contrasted the self-confidence and persuasion of a strong, life-loving hero.

He was always at the center of the artistic life of the 20th century and was well aware of its peculiarities—the motley succession of idols soon dethroned, the tendency towards thoughtless experimentation. The composer countered this volatile instability with the precious heritage of his teachers—a lofty art full of noble power. His music was a vehicle for the high ethical ideals that had, for centuries, inspired the best representatives of Russian art—the feeling of participation in the life of one's country, in its history, its destiny, its great culture. The composer's fascination with the themes, the artistic styles, and the folklore of other lands and ages, was a manifestation of that wonderful quality of Russian talents which Dostoyevsky referred to as "universal receptivity."

The composer's work was, above all, distinguished by purity of civic stance. "I hold the conviction," Prokofiev wrote, "that the composer's calling, like that of the poet, the sculptor, the artist, is to serve man and the people. He must make human life beautiful and defend it. He must, first of all, be a citizen in his art; he must glorify human life and lead man towards a bright future. Such is, I believe, the enduring code of art."

Prokofiev at work.

The perfection and classical precision of form, the strict logic of every movement and turn, the expressive imagery in Prokofiev's work are striking. His musical language, unique in its magical richness but also in its brevity and its chiseled completeness, reminds one of Shakespeare or Pushkin. Prokofiev's music, which has become a classic in our lifetime, will always be astonishingly modern. It was born of the 20th century, but its way lies into immortality...

The Boy From Sontzovka

The blinding golden sunlight, the vast carpets of heather, embroidered with the motley silk of field flowers; the ocean of wheat, swaying slightly in the wind; a lark high in the air over the magnificent luxury of summer. The Ukrainian land . . . Here, not far from Donetzk (it was called Yuzovka then and was a filthy, sooty miners' town), in a village by the ringing name of Sontzovka, Sergei Prokofiev was born ninety-two years ago, on April 11 (April 23, New Style) 1891.

From his early childhood, Prokofiev retained the memory of a beautiful, almost fantastic sight. A coach drawn by a foursome speeds along the steppe. A horseman gallops at the side of it, lighting the way with a torch. The mobile flame flashes with a streak of gold; the stark darkness is frightening; the stallions are breathing heavily. The family is coming back to Sontzovka from a long journey.

At the beginning of this century, Sontzovka is already a large and well-to-do village with a thousand inhabitants. It is a pleasure to walk along the streets, admiring the gifts of the Ukrainian soil growing and ripening in the orchards and in the fields. The landowner's large orchard is especially beautiful. The amazing novelties of agricultural technology have found their way here. Every year, new farm machines and seeds arrive; on one occasion, they even brought a breed of peacocks. But the exotic birds did not feel at ease among the noisy and impudent farm-fowls.

The village of Sontzovka.

Winter here is snowy, summer is hot. At night the black, star-spangled velvet sky hangs over the low houses, over the froth of the garden, silvery in the dark. At night the safety of Sontzovka is entrusted to the two night watchmen, Gavrilo and Mikhailo; they walk around the landlord's mansion with their clappers, or else they get drunk and sleep curled-up on a bench.

There is a church in the village, always crowded on Sundays; the people say the Vespers solemnly and ceremoniously on important holidays. Did Prokofiev's love for performances perhaps originate from those childhood years when his mother took him to church?

The Prokofievs' house is simple, sturdy, and squat. The rooms are low-ceilinged; there are flowerpots, massive furniture with

Mariya Grigorievna Prokofieva,
the composer's mother.

**Sergei Alexandrovich Prokofiev,
the composer's father.**

old upholstery concealed under covers. At the side of Father's bed, there is a huge steel box where keys to many barns are kept at night.

Of the three children born to Mariya Grigorievna and Sergei Alexeyevich Prokofiev, only one, Seryozha, survived. A late child, and an exceptionally gifted one, the boy was ardently loved by his parents and returned their love and devotion with the same intensity. "My mother was the most intellectual person in her family, as my father was in his," he later remembered with pride.

Sergei Alexeyevich Prokofiev, the son of a petty industrialist, decided in his youth not to follow his parents' profitable trade; he was attracted to science. After finishing school and college, he studied in the Petrovsko-Razumovskaya Academy of Agriculture in Moscow. Having accepted landowner Sontzov's proposal to manage his estate in the Ukraine, Prokofiev became in effect the master of the land. Pride and modesty made Sergei Alexeyevich avoid contact with the neighboring landowners. The Prokofievs lived in seclusion, but this alienation was brought on by their education and their intellectual superiority over the local gentry.

The large library in the house was continuously enriched. The interests of the head of the family were broad and diverse; Sergei Alexeyevich himself taught his son Russian, arithmetic, geography, history. "As a teacher, Father was meticulous and pedantic, but sometimes he would bring some joy into my existence, in the form of a piece of chocolate . . ."

Not only did the boy respect his father; he had a tender affection for him and never forgot his dignified and grave look or his ability, "even in his old age, to laugh irrepressibly as a child."

Sergei Prokofiev in 1898.

On a photo dated 1876, Mariya Grigorievna is scarcely more than twenty years old. Her dress is simple but elegant, her stature is noble, her face is not beautiful but remarkable. The wonderful eyes of this intelligent, dreamy woman have a kind and even helpless look—the latter probably a result of bad myopia, for Mariya Grigorievna was, generally speaking, a dominant and vigorous woman.

Manyasha Zhitkova grew up in a poor family and graduated from a Lyceum with a gold medal award; in 1877, she married Sergei Alexeyevich Prokofiev. She left Moscow with him and settled in Sontzovka; she became Mariya Grigorievna, a manager's wife, the mistress of a large estate, even though it was not her own; and she quickly adapted to her new role.

Contemporaries remember Mariya Grigorievna as a stimulating person with a keen and inquisitive mind. Fascinating and communicative, she knew, according to her son, how to "charm" people and win their sympathy. One can imagine how bored this active and energetic woman felt in a remote corner like Sontzovka, where she always had to think of crops, of cattle, of reports to the landowner. She dreamed of witty conversationalists, of refined and entertaining discussions, of travels. In her reveries she could see austere concert halls, crowded theatre boxes, the curtain rustling as it goes up. ". . . Such concepts as 'enlightenment,' 'progress,' 'science,' 'culture' were venerated by my parents more than anything, and were perceived as Enlightenment, Progress, Science, Culture with capital letters," the composer wrote. It was not only religious devotion but a passionate aspiration to spiritual values that was the meaning of her existence. Every trip to the city was packed with attendance at theatres and at recitals. Mariya Grigorievna dispelled the boredom of her endless leisure hours in Sontzovka by playing the piano six hours a day.

She also practiced philanthropy; she taught at a village school and gave medical treatment to the peasants. And, finally, the talent of her son, manifest at an early age, gave meaning to her life; in motherhood, she found her true vocation.

"Mother loved music, Father had a high regard for music," Prokofiev wrote in his *Autobiography*. "The amount of music that I had access to was tremendous." Mariya Grigorievna spent many hours playing piano, and, amazingly, her little son would sit in an armchair and listen to everything she played. "Mother, exercising in the middle register, sometimes conceded the two upper octaves to me, to tap out my childish experiments."

The age of five and a half is marked by the appearance of his first composition. A simple tune runs through the melody, persistently and merrily; the name, *A Hindu Galop,* reflected, in a curious way, the conversations of the adults as they discussed hunger in India.

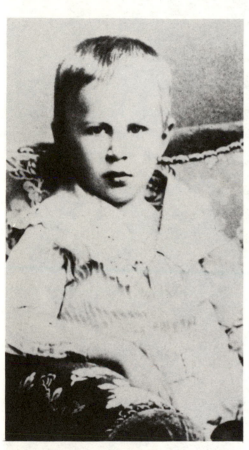

Little Seryozha listens to Mother playing the piano.

Sometimes, the boy tried to write down, or rather to draw, music himself. "I wrote it as ornament, as children draw little people and trains, for I often saw music on the music-stand." The boy's urge to compose required that Mariya Grigorievna explain to him the elementary basics of notation in music. Sometimes, it was his mother who wrote down his fantasies, coping with this new task "with some difficulty, never having done it before."

The first expressions of little Seryozha's talent were promising. There was no doubt that he was gifted and interested in music. The scowling child began to dominate, self-confidently and imperiously, the whole tenor and purpose of life in Sontzovka. The concerns of the family were now devoted exclusively to the boy's education in a rational, consistent, thoughtful, and demanding way.

A luxurious, spectacular Schroeder grand piano was brought into the house. "The Prokofievs are plain crazy," neighbors were saying. "What do they need another piano for?" When the parents made up their minds to hire a governess, Mariya Grigorievna went as far as Warsaw to find a native Frenchwoman, articulate in her language. Her son might, perhaps, wear his deceased little sister's clothes; but his teachers had to be better than those of the local landowners' children.

His first instructor was, of course, his own mother. She understood very well that to foster love of music, lessons had to be interesting. "Therefore: as little time as possible for exercising, and as much as possible for readings. An excellent method that every Mom should keep in mind." At first, lessons were no longer than 20 minutes; it was not until the age of nine that they gradually were expanded to an hour, with an obligatory discus-

Seryozha with his parents in their
Sontzovka garden.

"Aunt Tanya took me to a
photographer who took my picture
in front of a cardboard piano with
a blank sheet on the music stand.
When the pictures were ready,
they were taken to a co-worker of
Aunt Tanya's who had a
calligraphic handwriting, and he
skillfully made the inscription:
The Giant. An opera by Seryozha
Prokofiev.'"

sion of each new piece. The results of this wise teaching method were to be revealed in the near future.

A new century – 1900 – is coming, with its amazing changes. Every morning a Russian citizen opens his newspaper with trepidation, expecting more news—frightening, or happy, or baffling. A carefully planned farce is being staged in France—the Dreyfus case which brought the country to the brink of a civil war. A celebration of Leo Tolstoy's 70th birthday is banned in Russia.

Scientific progress is breathtaking. On the threshold of the new century, a device to transmit sound without wire, with the help of electromagnetic waves only, is demonstrated by A. Popov in Russia and by G. Marconi in the United States. C. Roentgen discovers the X-ray; the Curies discover radium and polonium. In 1897 K. Ader goes up in the air in his apparatus that looks like a giant bat and, having flown about a hundred feet, crashes. In 1900, the first subway train in Paris rattles along; the unfamiliar sound of the motor-car horn is heard in the streets of European and American cities.

The first films are produced in Russia. In 1896, the St. Petersburg public is invited to the "Aquarium" park for the viewing of a "foreign attraction" by the unfamiliar name of "cinema." In Moscow, the young singer Fyodor Shalyapin makes his debut in S. I. Mamontov's Russian Private Opera; in 1898, the Khudozhestvenny Theatre opens with the premiere of *Tsar Fyodor Ioannovich,* and in 1900 the premiere of Rimsky-Korsakov's new opera *The Tale of Tsar Saltan* enjoys a tremendous success. An exhibition of Russian and Finnish painters marks the beginning of the activities of the "Mir Iskusstva" ("World of Art") group; the first issue of the magazine by that name is published. On the cover, there is a picture of a proud eagle, his mighty wings spread wide over the vain things of this earth.

Prokofiev's first music manuscript.

Contemporaries are growing up. While Prokofiev is studying music notation with diligence, schoolboy Igor Stravinsky is introduced to Rimsky-Korsakov; Pablo Picasso's heart is first captured by Paris the year Seryozha hears *Faust* and *Sleeping Beauty*; and, when Sergei Prokofiev's daring recitals begin to shock the musical circles of St. Petersburg, high school student Sergei Eisenstein gets his first "C" in art.

On the eve of the 20th century, Sergei Prokofiev had his first glimpse of the life that he was to enter somewhat later: travels for thousands of miles, large cities, high art.

The boy's parents decided to celebrate the New Year 1900 with a trip to Moscow. The noisy capital blinded the boy with the unfamiliar brightness of electric lights, crushed him with the masses of magnificent buildings, deafened him with the yells of cabbies, with the clang of horse-trams. But it was not the Bolshoi Theatre, its square crowded with coaches, or Christ the Savior's majestic temple, or the exquisite beauty of the Kremlin, that made the greatest impression on the boy; it was theatre itself.

He was taken to *Faust*; he already knew the music from Mariya Grigorievna's performance at home. What he liked most was the duel, and also the scene of Valentine's death and Mephistopheles in a ray of red light. *Sleeping Beauty* in the Bolshoi literally made his head spin: "When they (that is, someone in *Sleeping Beauty*) were moving forward in their boat, and the moving stage set started gliding in the opposite direction, my captivated eyes looked around helplessly, and the theatre seemed to be swimming, too . . . and then I didn't know whether it was the stage, or the theatre, or just my head that was spinning."

The trip to Moscow gave a new meaning to the boy's life: the theatre entered with its mysteries, its fantasies, the fascination of its motley luxury. As a first step, he decided to . . . write an opera. Mariya Grigorievna's skepticism about this idea did not discourage him at all: " . . . At the age of ten, I already had my own point of view on musical works and could argue for it." In the beginning of that summer, the boy's mother had before her a pile of somewhat sloppy sheets of paper—the manuscript of the new opera, *The Giant*.

Through the uncomplicated and simple effects of this composition, one gets a glimpse of the composer's future individuality: a tendency toward forceful means of expression and strongly marked contrasts. The musical vocabulary, slightly imitative of Gounod, is naive and not original, but on the other hand, the young composer strove to achieve stage effects. Here is a sample: the King, sitting in his balcony, resolves to give Sergeyev, the hero, a detachment of soldiers to destroy the evil Giant. And, at the same time, the Giant appears from nowhere, passes under the balcony and sings, together with the King: "They want to murder me!"

Next summer, *The Giant* was performed on the estate of the boy's uncle, A. D. Rayevsky. By that time, the sloppy scribbling had been copied by the governess and bound in a cover, with the title "THE GIANT, an opera in three acts composed by Seryozhenka Prokofiev."

The young members of the Rayevsky family, led by the author of the opera himself, searched through all the storerooms looking for sets and costumes. Parts were distributed and learned, though a little bit shakily. The adoring parents were delighted by the performance of the first act, and Uncle said, "Well, Seryozha, when your works are performed on the royal stage, just remember your first opera was produced in my house!"

Prokofiev remembered that twenty years later, when he saw a glittering crowd—in topcoats, diamonds, laces, sable mantles—stream into the black space of the Chicago Opera hall, and the enormous golden-red letters on the poster in the foyer: *A Love for Three Oranges*.

The first successful experiment in the field of opera was followed by more attempts: throughout 1901, the boy worked at an opera with an adventure subject, *On Desert Isles*. The libretto was packed with extraordinary events, storms, shipwrecks. But the author's turbulent fantasy was locked in a dead end, and the composition did not go beyond the first act, when the heroes find themselves on a desert island . . .

The boy was growing up, and his education in music had to be

A fragment from *The Giant*.
Autograph.

considered seriously. In December 1901, the family went to Moscow and to St. Petersburg again. At their friends' home in Moscow, the Prokofievs met a young musician Yu. N. Pomerantzev. He promised to arrange for them to be introduced to his teacher Taneyev, who was "the very top professor in Moscow."

The professor lived in a modest apartment which a few years later he exchanged for another one just as modest. When numerous visitors, mostly budding composers and pupils, pestered him too much, he would hang a sign on the front door saying: "S. I. Taneyev is ill and does not see anyone. The bell is not working." Those were his working hours. There was no such sign displayed on January 23; Sergei Ivanovich was waiting for little Seryozha.

The furniture was simple, even scant; the old grand piano was lighted by an oil lamp. Mariya Grigorievna became nervous: "There was an air of something extraordinary, something unearthly about this room; the piles of music and books, the solitude, the silence and even the benign voice of the host overawed one, as if you were entering a temple."

Taneyev received the boy cordially and treated him to chocolate. Here are several entries in his journal: "Around two o'clock, Yusha (Yu. N. Pomerantzev) came for dinner. He brought a ten-year-old boy with him—Seryozha Prokofiev, who is exceptionally gifted. He played his own compositions. He has an absolute pitch, a recognition of chords and intervals." *February 3.* "I went over to Yusha to tell him to send little Seryozha Prokofiev a message that I can take him to a rehearsal." *February 4.* "Today, the rehearsal of my symphony with the strings. I sat close to little Seryozha Prokofiev, explaining to him all the details of score notation." *February 6.* "A rehearsal of my symphony with the complete orchestra. Conussek Catoire, Yusha, the Sabaneyevs, little Prokofiev, Eigess, Goldenveiser were there." *March 7.* "At 1 o'clock, the rehearsal of the Litvinov concerto (Pyotr Ilyich Tchaikovsky's Symphony No. 2, part one in the original version); . . . From there, I went to Yusha's place, to test little Prokofiev on harmony."

The Bolshoi Theatre in Moscow (early 1900s).

Sergei Ivanovich recommended that a professional musician be hired to stay in Sontzovka during the summer as instructor to Seryozha. He found such an instructor, too—Reinhold Moritzevich Glier, a young composer who had just graduated from the conservatory with a gold medal.

In June 1902 the whole family was preparing excitedly to meet the teacher.

Glier had thick black hair, a moustache, a violin in his hands. He stooped a little, his face had a grave look, but the eyes, set wide apart under bushy eyebrows, were ready to smile at any moment. He managed to gain the boy's love, for even his slightly old-fashioned politeness could not conceal the fact that he was essentially kind, simple and hearty, just as was his music. The young instructor was a man of few words, but that was no obstacle to their friendship; whenever help or advice was needed, he revealed himself as a generous and magnanimous person.

Glier participated in many of the boy's childish games, treating his as yet uncomplicated theatrical amusements very seriously; the next summer, during Glier's second stay, they worked together enthusiastically on the composition of Seryozha's third opera, *The Feast During the Plague*.

Explaining musical forms and harmony, Glier roused the interest and the curiosity of his pupil. The method of becoming familiar with the basics of instrumentation was "picturesque enough": "While we were practicing the piano in the morning, he would spot a passage or a melody characteristic of one instrument or another in a Beethoven sonata or some other piece, and then stop and tell me that, if that piece were orchestrated, this strong-sounding triad would be played by three trombones, this pastoral melody, by an oboe, and this melodious middle note should be given to a cello." What both the pupil and the teacher loved most was improvisation. Glier executed colorful virtuoso improvisations on folk-song themes, while Seryozha preferred themes of his own.

Glier introduced a useful practice: an assignment, every month, to compose a short piano piece. The miniatures were called "songs" and usually were composed on the occasion of a major or minor holiday in the family, so many of them are dedicated to a person: "Dedicated to dear Papa by S. Prokofiev, 28.3. 1904," to "Aunt Tanechka," to "Godfather." He wrote twelve in a year, and from 1902 to 1906, there were 60. It was time to catalogue his own work . . .

"Most respected Sergei Ivanovich!

"Recently, Reinhold Moritzevich has left our house, leaving the best memory behind him. He is irreplaceable as an instructor. He has so much tact and patience! With his knowledge and love of music, he could always get Seryozha interested and incline him to composition. Seryozha's summer compositions, written under Reinhold Moritzevich's supervision, are quite different. One can feel Seryozha has been set on the right track.

"For all this I must express my deepest gratitude to you, most respected Sergei Ivanovich. My husband and Seryozha join me. We all thank you very sincerely and with all our souls.

"This year, I shall try to make arrangements so that we can go to Moscow twice, as you have advised, a month before Christmas and a month after; meanwhile, we shall work on our own, blindly groping.

"I wish you the best; and, with the fullest and deepest respect for you, sincerely yours

Mariya Prokofieva
September 11, 1902"

Of course, she succeeded in arranging a trip to Moscow a month before Christmas.

In November, Seryozha, now a year older, brought to Taneyev seven songs and a symphony—the crown of his creative achievement in the first summer of studies with Glier. It was played in four hands, "he and I, Taneyev doing humbly the left hand." Sergei Ivanovich praised the symphony, but remarked in his usual mocking tone, "Bravo, bravo! But the harmonization is still

Autograph of a symphony written under the instruction of Glier. Inscribed (in 1945) "to Reinhold Moritzevich on the wonderful day of his 70th birthday, with memories of our first meeting in 1902."

rather primitive. Mostly . . . ha, ha . . . the first and the fourth and the fifth steps!" The ambitious boy was deeply mortified and remembered the "ha, ha" for quite a long time. Prokofiev later linked, at least in part, his subsequent love for experimentation and innovation in the field of harmonic language with that memorable visit to Taneyev.

In Moscow, mother and son attended many concerts. They heard Shalyapin, Nikisch, organ music. The boy liked Beethoven and Grieg. *Die Walküre*, performed in the Bolshoi, did not appeal to him: "A terribly boring opera, without motives, without dynamic, but with a lot of noise." He came to love Wagner later, and, after a few years, it was the piano score for this opera that he chose as a Christmas gift from his parents.

Seryozha did not attend a remarkable premiere in Moscow that took place the day before Nikisch's concert. On December 12, as if to compensate for the failure of the composer's previous opera, *Servilia*, the Muscovites received enthusiastically Rimsky-Korsakov's *Kashchey the Immortal.* Tempest the Knight, with his chromatic orchestra passages, Kashcheyevna and her charmed sword, the ominous "creeping" harmonies in Kashchey's part, the liberation of prisoners, the fall of Kashchey's kingdom—all of that would doubtless have impressed the receptive boy. But in those days Seryozha was busy and did not hear *Kashchey.*

The spring and the summer of 1905 were spent in tireless work. The boy practiced harmony, collected plants, and, for some reason, to his mother's amazement, counted the number of bars in *Eugene Onegin.* In autumn, parallel to his work at *The Feast During the Plague,* new "trifles" in the romance genre appear. Some of them are serious, poems by Pushkin and Lermontov set to music; one is facetious, dedicated to Leonid Sobinov.

Since the winter of 1904, the parents worried about the problem of the boy's further education. After much deliberation and many arguments, they chose the St. Petersburg Conservatory. Mariya Grigorievna took her son to St. Petersburg, where they became acquainted with Alexander Konstantinovich Glazunov. The famous composer finally persuaded the mother, who was still in doubt, to send her son to the conservatory: "It is at the Conservatory that his talent will be fully developed, and there's a good chance of his becoming a real artist."

Sergei Taneyev with Yuri Pomerantzev, Prokofiev's harmony teacher.

Meanwhile, musical impressions were refreshed, new ideas were conceived. At a performance of *The Snow-Maiden,* the curious boy who watched the scores while leaning over the edge of the orchestra pit, attracted the attention of a lady sitting next to him. It was Mariya Grigorievna Kilshett, an amateur poetess. She offered Seryozha a subject for a new opera, *Ondine,* after F. Lamotte-Fouquet; he agreed, and she set to writing the libretto.

The family went back to Sontzovka with grand new plans. The boy's last summer at home was occupied with intense preparations for the exams, with composing the *Ondine* (he would complete the opera later, in 1907). The family had to separate, for he could not live in St. Petersburg without his mother, and his father could not leave the estate. It was decided that the family would reunite at home for the vacations, and during the academic terms the father would visit his wife and son in St. Petersburg. It gave Sergei Alexeyevich some pain to agree to this arrangement; the fifty-eight-year-old man did not want to part from his family and remain alone. But there was no other choice. In August 1904 Mariya Grigorievna took her son to St. Petersburg. Seryozha bade farewell to Sontzovka in a joyous mood, for he "was not afraid of the exams, looked forward to many exciting things; and Father was going to come in a month."

Childhood was over, ended in a rather abrupt way, and by the time he entered the Conservatory, the chubby, fair-haired boy from the Ukraine was no longer just an infant prodigy, but a fully formed personality. St. Petersburg would open before him the doors into the world of great music; he would learn new skills, his willpower would be fortified, his style polished. But the capital would never change what he already had—an exceptionally strong nature, a responsiveness to the beautiful and a hatred for everything primitive, trite, mediocre.

His personality—as it was throughout his life—was not simple but even perhaps contradictory. People close to the family remembered him as a gentle and sweet boy, with a great deal of affection for his parents. But after some unsuccessful practice in four-hand music with his mother, who lagged behind significantly in piano technique, he would leave her tearful at the piano and run away to play with his toys.

In a surprising way, he combined earnestness, diligence, willpower, and hard work with a perpetual inclination to pranks, fancy, naughtiness. He studied with great ease, and so music was, for him, a source of joy never clouded by rote learning, punishments and failures. A highly developed critical sense, seasoned with irony, helped him preserve his individuality and independent views. The young provincial argued heatedly with the fifty-year-old worldly poetess, insisting on cuts in the exceedingly lengthy libretto for *Ondine*. In letters to his father from the capital, he pronounced confident and well-argued judgment on music he had heard. This was done more in an effort to emphasize the independence of his own opinions than an endeavor toward the truth. But independence was evident: "On Monday, we saw *The Queen of Spades*. It's a good opera, but the singing, the acting and the stage sets are revolting."

He was proud of his talent; he showed off his compositions and played willingly and lavishly, never fearing evaluations. His parents probably did not disapprove of aplomb—at any rate, that is the word Mariya Grigorievna used in her reminiscences when describing his never-ending piano improvisations before guests. He grew up in an atmosphere of adoration on the part of his elderly parents, his grandmother, his neighbors, his lonely aunt Tanya who took his early compositions to St. Petersburg to have them bound in red and gold covers. A clerk, Vanka, ruled music paper for him, a governess copied his sloppy scrawl. His pride was limitless. He took losses in tennis, chess or cricket very pain-

Reinhold Moritzevich Glier.

fully ("once, left the playground in tears"), but respected a strong adversary. He was sociable and friendly. In letters to his father, he inquired with concern, "How are the children? Do they walk on the stilts? I hope they haven't broken them, and I hope they don't quarrel and fight over them. Do they feed the dogs?" He sent Christmas greetings to "Marfusha, and also Motrya, Yelena, Nikita, Yekaterina, Stenya, Seryozha, Vasya . . ." And they, those who had stayed in Sontzovka, missed him.

In his earliest works, despite his total trust in Glier, he still strove to be independent. "I wanted to compose something bold, with no one holding me by the coattails." Four operas and a symphony, for which he sometimes had to defend his right to compose, are a proof of the triumph of this determination. Even then, when composing, he tried to preserve the logic of scenic truth. About the *Ondine,* he remarked: ". . . How was the stream which I have regarded as a formidable natural phenomenon, frightening to the knight and the fisherman, to evolve into an innocent and delicate dance of little founts?" He was interested in the characters' personalities, in the psychological motives of their behavior. In the script of the never-staged dramatic episode *People,* the heroes perish because of a conflict of incompatible personalities and the inability to speak the same language.

The boy composed music unselfconsciously, enthusiastically, as if playing a game; many ideas for his early works were born in the process of play, such as, for instance, the most scenic episodes of *The Giant.* At the same time, he engaged in his boyish pursuits seriously, like a researcher, making careful notes, calculations, diagrams. Among his hobbies were: studying train schedules of Russian railroads, collecting plants and stamps, writing a novel in verse, and a tract on stilts.

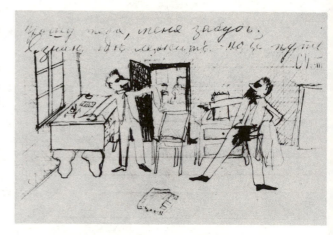

Another literary work of Prokofiev's childhood, *The Count,* consisted of quartrains, each illustrated by the author.

Let us look at two notebooks his mother gave to him as gifts. They contain the entire world of the boy's joys and cares. There is a neat table of contents at the end. Let us choose just some titles at random: "The best type of battleship" (a detailed study backed up with calculations and drafts), "Another way of calculating the battle coefficient of battleships," "Card gambling," "Stilts contests," "Solutions of rebuses and charades," "Tournament results" (concerning not only chess but shooting with toy pistols —something in which Glier, too, gladly engaged).

"Chess games I have played (1906)." Players: Marfusha vs. S. Prokofiev (often without a rook).

"The lifetime of composers. A double line indicates the years of the composer's creative work (a diagram)."

There is also the boy's highest literary achievement: a comedy in three acts about a persistent debtor, "wicked Sasheyev," about his foul murder, about witty crooks and the final triumph of virtue embodied by a policeman who solemnly arrests the felons as the curtain goes down.

Creativity and play ignite each other as they come close. Creativity always verges on play—inventive, accurately planned, "scientific" play; the line that separates them is often intangible. Is not this diversity combining creativity, play and rationality another thread that binds Prokofiev firmly to the 20th century?

A variety of interests, the ability to engage in many pursuits, are qualities Prokofiev retained throughout his life. The childhood years lay the foundation for his remarkable personal and artistic discipline. For that, one cannot exaggerate his mother's contribution. Strict but never tyrannical, affectionate but demanding, she was always able to understand her son's yearnings and to let him exercise his own initiative freely. She taught the boy to evaluate every day of his life by asking him two questions in the evening: "What have you done today?" and "Are you satisfied with what you have done?" Throughout his life, Prokofiev retained the need to work with a fanatic's enthusiasm and a craftsman's precision.

Drawing of a battle at sea, from Prokofiev's childhood notebook.

Rimsky-Korsakov, one of the towering figures in Russian and world music at the turn of the century.

Great Russian composer and
musician Alexander Glazunov.

Sergei Prokofiev as a Conservatory
student.

The Student of the St. Petersburg Conservatory

On September 9, 1904, there was an admission exam on a special subject. A stately lady led the golden-haired boy by the hand. Usually merry and active, he was somewhat subdued in this unfamiliar stern atmosphere, but he looked around with curiosity and with no fear. He was not worried about the coming exam, but noted and remembered everything, so that he could describe it in detail in the next letter to his father. People taking exams in special theory are usually adult. One of them later expressed his bewilderment: "I am over thirty and have two children, and Prokosha is just thirteen."

The committee included N. A. Rimsky-Korsakov, A. K. Glazunov, A. K. Lyadov. The examiners were pleased with the way the thirteen-year-old read music fluently, recognized keys and chords accurately, singing true in his breaking boyish voice. The thing that impressed them most was the young composer's striking fecundity: four operas, a symphony, two sonatas and many piano pieces. The past year's works were piled separately; and, there was also a list of his compositions.

Sergei Prokofiev was admitted to A. K. Lyadov's harmony class. And so he appeared in the conservatory—"a tall mobile boy, very blond, with lively eyes, a nice complexion and a generous mouth, very neatly dressed and combed. He looked very dignified." Prokofiev's classmate Vera Alpers in her memoirs included, in addition to this description, her impressions of his personality. He was outstanding among students in general-education classes for his learning, which instantly earned him their respect. His determination to have his own opinion on everything grew even stronger, and the boy acquired the reputation of a spirited fellow. His judgments were extremely sharp, and his straightforwardness, his persistence in searching out the truth about everything, his unwillingness to avoid conflicts made many of those he criticized unsympathetic. While studying in Lyadov's class, he carefully noted his classmates' mistakes in harmony exercises and kept an accurate statistical table at home, which infuriated his fellow students. Yet despite his rashness, his perky and defiant manner, his perpetual questioning of

The building of the St. Petersburg Conservatory.

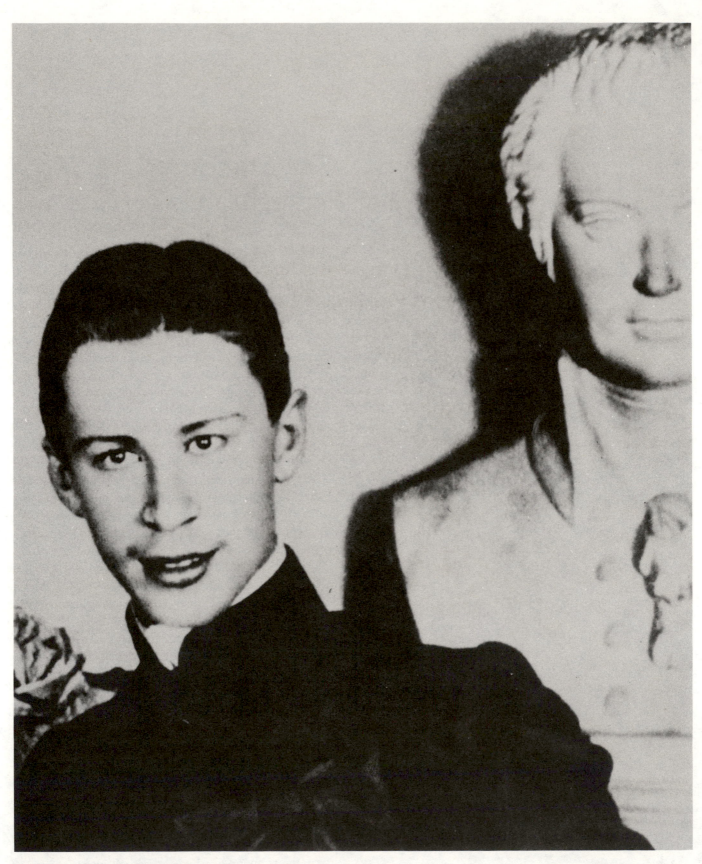

Prokofiev at a Conservatory ball.

Prokofiev's lifelong friend Nikolai
Myaskovsky in his youth.

authorities, he was singled out in the Conservatory for his talent, his thirst for knowledge, his quick response to things, his marvellous sense of humor. He was loved and feared a little.

In the early 1900s, the St. Petersburg Conservatory was the magnetic center that drew the musical youth of Russia. Among the Conservatory's leading professors were Russian musicians of world renown: N. A. Rimsky-Korsakov, A. K. Glazunov, A. K. Lyadov. Yet the stifling atmosphere of bureaucracy and conventionality which seemed to penetrate into all areas of life in imperial St. Petersburg, also poisoned the daily life in the Conservatory. Its formal director, the mediocre musician August Bernhard, "had no idea of the heights of art" and had no authority with the musicians.

The dull gray humdrum life was intolerable to those who yearned for great art and, to come here, had left behind the comfortable idleness of well-to-do families, important positions with a steady income, studies in other more material sciences that promised prosperity in the future. "What if we take from this museum of music its soul that performed miracles of devotion in it: Rimsky-Korsakov and Glazunov, and with them several prominent artist/teachers like Yessipova and Auer—will not this enormous cold building become just an empty case without a violin?"— Asafiev wrote.

From the very beginning, Prokofiev's relationships with his teachers were not easy. The never-ending conflicts within the Conservatory were caused by more than the oppressive humdrum atmosphere and the inspectors' supervision, the strict order under which one had to "listen and obey." The many-sided and complicated processes, the breathtaking changes that were happening in art at the turn of the century left their mark on some teachers' attitude to modern music in which they perceived a destructive force. Students yearned for the new, protested fiercely against what seemed academically old-fashioned and primitively "straitlaced." As a result, there were feelings of alienation, of mutual grudges. The students' complex relationship with Lyadov is an example.

. . . Anatoly Konstantinovich Lyadov. A brilliant master of artistic form, a rare fanciful inventor, a musician of incorruptible artistic conscience who, throughout his life, longed for beauty, searched for it, created it in his few miniatures. The ear-scratching harmonies, the broken lines of chaotically moving voices in the scores of new composers made him suffer; from the depths of his heart, he rebelled against this art that he perceived as a barbaric apotheosis of confusion, loudness, artificial high-flown pretentiousness.

But with the same intolerance, Lyadov protested against lazy and mediocre rehashing of traditions, against everything ordinary, rote-learned, trite. One of his favorite slogans was: "Learn to hinder everything habitual in yourself!" In his *Autobiography*, Prokofiev describes how Lyadov "raved" at the composition finals, and "through the door, left slightly ajar, one could hear his screams, 'They all want to be Scriabins, and what

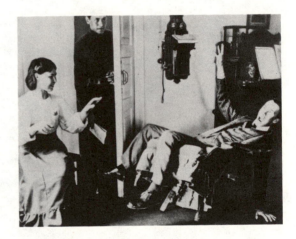

Despite Sergei's eagerness to learn, there was more to his life than studying and attending concerts: here, the boy is shown in a comedy sketch with friends.

is it that they bring to the exams?'" And yet Lyadov's letters of approximately the same period are full of tireless yearning for innovation: "I am painfully thirsty for everything new and extraordinary . . ." "Only 'novelty' brings me joy." ". . . I am so happy new people with 'new' ideas become more visible. I am awfully tired of the old."

Young composers were burningly impatient to write new music, and expected their teachers to introduce them to this music with the same inspiration and enthusiasm that they felt while listening to it in the gallery of a concert or theatre hall, their heads colliding in the dark, quarreling in an angry whisper over the one, difficult-to-obtain score.

Lyadov did not perceive in the bold, disobedient pupils the "new ones" he was waiting for. They looked up to him as a mentor, and he turned out to be "so terribly conservative!" And they went away disappointed, remembering his tired indifference, his sarcastic fault-finding, his hatred of their new idols.

Alexander Scriabin, one of the most controversial composers of the 1900s, was a powerful influence on Prokofiev in his adolescence.

"With a squeamish mien, speaking through set teeth, Lyadov . . . drew an example on the blackboard . . . and with a peculiar lazy grace, with an expression of suffering on his face, played the students' exercises on the piano, fishing out all the slop in an incomparable way." Lyadov was tired. Every day, he came to the Conservatory and spent six hours there, and then went home only to receive more pupils. He had started to teach at the Conservatory before his graduation, and for twenty-three years he had been teaching required theory subjects to pianists, singers, violinists. His pupils, indifferent to his classes, often simply illiterate, filled the composer with disgust for teaching. "I think of the Conservatory with horror: E major has four sharps, what will *C-E* be? etc. And this, for the rest of my life!" When, in 1901, the composer was finally assigned a special course in counterpoint and fugue, and later, a course in practical composition, he had no more enthusiasm or strength left to introduce the mysteries of musical creativity to young composers. And thirteen-year-old Sergei Prokofiev also had to be taught the connection between harmony exercises and the music he was going to write.

Lyadov taught the beauty and purity of exquisitely refined writing, the art of well-proportioned balance between all the components of a musical whole. His relentless insistence on abiding by rules verged on despotism; his highly developed taste spared nothing, not even scores of famous composers, and his hatred of musical "slop" of which his pupils' works were so full compelled him to hide behind an impenetrable armor of irony. His unjust pupils saw only his arrogant lordly appearance, and did not recognize the suffering in his eyes; they heard the hostility in his voice, and were unwilling to admire the beauty and precision of his speech in which the poet Sergei Gorodetzky delighted ("His words were like pieces of flint"); irritated, they corrected errors in counterpoint that he had pointed out—and could not resolve the contradiction between Lyadov's fault-finding and his own words, "But all the charm of art consists in the masterful transgression of rules, in these pranks of the im-

Anatoly Lyadov, an outstanding
mind torn between traditionalism
and yearning for the new.

Boris Asafiev, a fellow student of
Prokofiev's and later, one of the
most perceptive and profound
commentators on his music.

agination." Seeing him tired and bored, they did not know that outside the classroom, the man was witty and sharp, wrote sarcastic epigrams. And, tired of boring exercises, they forgot all about the exquisite charm of his music, its perfect beauty and its novelty, the novelty they wanted and missed in his classes.

His complaints about Prokofiev ("He knows the rules but makes errors when he writes; he has no self-criticism.) and others, conscientiously recalled in the *Autobiography*, were still lit by a ray of hope. Asafiev told Prokofiev, "Lyadov said about you that, even though he finds your music disgusting, still your talent will break out." Time showed that Lyadov's influence on Prokofiev's creative growth proved to be much more considerable than he could ever have supposed in his student years. An amazing tenderness, the chastity of lyrical passages, a refined precision, the sharpness of writing in the miniatures, and, finally, the wise kindness of a smiling story-teller—these are the traits of Prokofiev's creative personality that undoubtedly linked him to his teachers, the classics of Russian music.

In St. Petersburg, the mother and the son rented an apartment at 90 Sadovaya Street, near the church of the Holy Mother's Shroud. The apartment was small and not too comfortable, but for Mariya Grigorievna this place in St. Petersburg was a symbol of an earned, well-deserved better life. The wife of the manager of Sontzovka finally had a long-desired "circle of acquaintances" in the capital, her son a successful Conservatory student. Furniture, the piano, servants—everything required money, but Mariya Grigorievna, displaying miracles of invention, devoted herself totally to arranging their new life. Seryozha had a room of his own, with a large desk, among the desirable features of which were drawers with locks. Mother and son immersed themselves enthusiastically in big-city life. They took trips to the picturesque suburbs with their delightful combinations of fancy palaces and stern Nordic scenery. The boy acquired bizarre clockwork toys, though the temptation of the St. Petersburg stores was sometimes quelled by the indomitable will of his thrifty mother. At the home of their relatives, the Rayevskys, descendants of the glorious general, Seryozha was initiated into the mysteries of high-society manners; Mariya Grigorievna took him to the home of Dr. Pototzky, a surgeon, for dancing lessons. The future author of immortal ballets stamped clumsily with the doctor's daughter, to a hired pianist's strumming. "I didn't dance too gracefully," he remarked. Forty years later, Eisenstein will agree: "When Prokofiev himself dances, he always steps on ladies' feet. He is so much used to the disintegration of rhythm that ordinary, normal human rhythm is difficult for him; his feet can't catch up with it."

The amazing thing was that the Prokofiev family persisted as a solid entity. Trips were often taken from Sontzovka to St. Petersburg; letters were exchanged even more frequently, for they shared even the little things with each other. On her birthday, Mariya Grigorievna wrote to her husband: "Dinner was good, and so was everything. We drank to your health and called

This picture of young Prokofiev actually consists of two photographs— one taken with his face and the other taken with his back to the camera, then cut out and pasted together.

out 'Hurray!' to you many times as we clinked our glasses—you must have heard!" Seryozha missed his father in particular: "I think of you every day . . . I wish you were living with us."

These low moods were brought about by the variety of St. Petersburg impressions that were forming his mental outlook.

Igor Stravinsky, who grew up in St. Petersburg several years earlier than Prokofiev, absorbed the sounds and smells of the big city, could intone and transcribe a tinker's yell in the street, remembered and rendered the sounds of an accordion, the scenes of merriment at a carnival fair—men strumming balalaikas, girls, their cheeks rouged with beet-juice, boys who dance squatting.

Prokofiev's talent matured in a different environment. The Conservatory library, where short Fribus, whose nickname was "Diminished fifth," after much insistence let him hold a newly issued piano or orchestral score of some new work. The austere Conservatory classroom "under the clock," was remembered for the frictions at Lyadov's difficult lessons, and later, for Rimsky-Korsakov's strict instructions. The enormous, elongated Big Hall of the Conservatory closed in the semicircle of the wall. If one looks down from the galleries, it is easy to imagine that this is really a dock, which one of those proud, beautiful ships that were destroyed at Tsushima may enter at any moment. Sounds of music fill the hall—and the vision created by the youth's imagination disappears . . .

At the turn of the century, St. Petersburg was rich in interesting concerts and plays. New works by Wagner, Richard Strauss, Debussy, Ravel were widely performed. Prokofiev was excited by Scriabin's fiery, eager "flight," by Beethoven's noble austerity, by the luxuriousness of the mighty Wagnerian orchestra. Inventive Reger gave an example of audacious, convincing logic of combining distant consonances; Rachmaninov's melodies stunned with their extraordinary plasticity and beauty. When he entered a period of firm, durable devotion to contemporary music, Prokofiev's creative radicalism induced him to compose music "on two fronts"—for demonstration in Lyadov's class, and for himself.

One of the idols of the time was Rimsky-Korsakov, a teacher revered deeply and with awe, an admired author of much-loved operas, the patriarch of Russian music, an audacious innovator who opened new ways for many musicians of the 20th century, including Prokofiev. With every bar of his scores, he illustrated the sublime synthesis of pure, skillful, "correct" writing and free flight of fantasy, brilliant invention, astounding truth and beauty.

The echo of the thundering storms of the first Russian revolution resounded many times in the Conservatory classes. Students gathered at meetings in support of the strike movement in the colleges of St. Petersburg, and early on the morning of March 16, a crowd of strikers surrounded the Conservatory. The students justly demanded lower tuition charges, organization of a mutual assistance bank, elimination of inspectorial supervision, distribution of free tickets for theatre and concerts. The administration responded by calling upon the police for

Cartoon sketch of German composer and conductor Max Reger, whose performances in St. Petersburg drew the attention of young Sergei Prokofiev.

help. One hundred and sixteen students were arrested, many strike activists expelled.

In those days, leading professors sided with the turbulent student body. In his letter to Bernhard, Rimsky-Korsakov sharply criticized not only the administration's actions, but the very system of management in the Conservatory. "Can there be any artistic-musical achievement in an institution where the decisions of the Artistic Council have no power; in an institution where, according to the statutes, musical artists are subordinated to the administration, that is, to a group of dilettante amateurs; in an institution where, according to the same statutes, the director is not elected for a term but appointed indefinitely; in an institution totally indifferent to the interests of the students in all educational issues?" On the insistence of several professors, Bernhard had to resign; three days later, a resolution that seemed almost incredible was passed. The administration of the St. Petersburg chapter of the Russian Musical Society dismissed Rimsky-Korsakov from his Conservatory chair. Glazunov, Lyadov, Verzhbilovich, Blumenfeld reacted to this revolting lawless ruling by announcing their resignations. Yessipova, who was touring abroad, sent an open letter to the press, refusing to continue her work in the Conservatory. Russian newspapers often quoted Yuli Engel's indignant words: "Music does not reside among those who are capable of such a folly as to 'fire' Rimsky-Korsakov; music is where he, great artist and teacher, is."

On March 27, the composer's pupils produced a performance of *Kashchey the Immortal*. The performance became a "unique, grandiose, overwhelmingly powerful public demonstration," Aleksandr Ossovsky recalled. Prokofiev did not attend the first night, but he had heard and admired the opera at the rehearsal. He was too young to recognize and understand the true meaning of what was happening in Russia. Most probably, it was a sense of comradeship that prompted him to sign his name to a letter that a group of students wrote to declare that they were leaving the Conservatory. But—"this is the first time I have joined a political protest."

He spent the summer of 1904 in quiet Sontzovka. Life on the estate was peaceful as usual, with all its attendant worries about the harvest, while the peasants of nearby villages were burning down landlords' houses. "The alarm-bell would wake me up, a great flame·glowing in the dark Southern night." That summer was marked by a memorable acquaintance with a young veterinarian Vassily Mitrofanovich Morolev. A passionate music-lover, he was won over by Seryozha's talent. The friends' meetings in Morolev's hospitable home were devoted to music, chess, endless conversations about art.

Conservatory life stagnated after the 1904 revolution; the best teachers were gone. Prokofiev took private lessons with Lyadov, at home. By the spring of 1906, the situation was normalized. Rimsky-Korsakov, Lyadov, Glazunov (now director) and other professors returned to the Conservatory.

In 1906 Rimsky-Korsakov undertook to teach a course of

A cartoon commenting on the dismissal of Rimsky-Korsakov: the celebrated musician is shown taking the Conservatory building away with him.

special instrumentation that had been discontinued twenty years before, and Prokofiev was one of his last pupils.

For young Prokofiev, Rimsky-Korsakov was a living legend. The young man loved to come to the Conservatory a little early and look out of the first-story window, waiting for Rimsky-Korsakov to appear. Tall and trim, the composer walked across the empty square at a steady, unhurried pace. At moments when Rimsky-Korsakov was carried away speaking about something, Sergei found his energetic face beautiful and picturesque. "I looked at him admiringly, thinking: here is a man who has achieved real success and fame!"

Working with the students, Rimsky-Korsakov revealed the mysterious depths of his remarkable mastery, scattering sparks of the precious fire of creativity. His comments, remarks, even his fault-finding outlined the shape of the complete, consistent system of the great master's artistic world-view. But to the fifteen-year-old boy, the teacher's assignments often seemed boring; the four-hour classes were tiring. "Even though Rimsky-Korsakov was the most interesting person among the Conservatory teachers, his class was far from being the most interesting."

Prokofiev may have considered classes of little use, but Rimsky-Korsakov's music reigned over everything that was heard in St. Petersburg.

February, 1907. The premiere of *The Tale Of The Invisible City of Kitezh And Fevronya The Maiden*. It was exceedingly difficult to get to the dress rehearsal, but Prokofiev was among the first at the theatre door. He listened to *The Tale of Kitezh* from the galleries and from the expensive parterre seats, alone and with his father who was visiting, following the music in the newly-printed score, anticipating with delight each favorite fragment of the opera he knew well in all the details.

The stage sets were designed by A. Vasnetzov and K. Korovin, and, even though the famous artists had not been able fully to render the unique charm of Rimsky-Korsakov's music, the Eden-like garden with bizarre trees and flowers that appears before the audience was magnificently beautiful. On stage was the famous opera singer Nadezhda Ivanovna Zabela. She had been an incomparable Snow-Maiden, but could not cope with a leading part any longer; her voice had faded and weakened. The small part of Sirin the Bird was given to her: ". . . Please, when distributing the parts, do not forget me, give me the Sirin part; you must agree that I have beaten the record in all the bird and fish things." The opera was dominated by the unforgettable character of Grishka Kuterma, performed by Ivan Yershov. This frightening, miserable, cowardly and brash drunkard, his eyes dim, his face bruised in a fight, became, in theatre history, the symbol of dark, suffering Russia . . .

In the fall of 1906, in Lyadov's class, Prokofiev met a new student—military engineer Nikolai Yakovlevich Myaskovsky. What, one wonders, could they have in common—a slim, handsome twenty-five-year-old ensign and a perky fifteen-year-old, a self-described "puppy"? It is hard to imagine a more unlikely com-

Prokofiev having a game of chess with his older friend, the veterinarian Vassily Morolev.

bination. The latter grew up as an only child in a family where all other interests were secondary to the nurturing of his talent. The former lost his mother early and spent his childhood years in a military school. The latter, at the age of five, wrote his compositions in a bold scrawl which immediately became the pride of his family, relatives, friends. A catalogue of his works was compiled when he was eleven; at the age of thirteen, he was known to Taneyev, Glazunov, Rimsky-Korsakov, Glier. The former wrote his first compositions at the age of fifteen; and seven years later, when he met Taneyev, he was too shy to show him his works. A strict discipline and the ability to work twelve hours a day made it possible for Myaskovsky to become, even as a young man, a musician of broad and varied interests and rare erudition.

Like all shy people, Nikolai Yakovlevich seemed to be protected outwardly by an armor of polite inaccessibility; but when he held his hand out to someone, he revealed a responsive and endlessly generous nature, a soul capable of deep feelings.

Myaskovsky had known of Prokofiev before. At one of Rachmaninov's rehearsals of his Piano Concerto no. 2, Nikolai Yakovlevich had spoken to his friend V. V. Yakovlev about the boy sitting next to Glier, and called him a promising composer. That must have happened in 1902 . . . Now, their friendship started with a yellow notebook of piano pieces that succeeded the now-ended series of "little songs." Myaskovsky took an interest in the pieces and returned them to Prokofiev with a remark that could but flatter the bold adolescent: "So this is the little snake we've cherished in our bosom!"

Maurice Ravel.

The obvious differences between these two people, the age gap, the differences in education and lifestyle did not prevent them from growing close to each other. Pure and idealistic attitudes towards art, the ability to work selflessly and, moreover, the outstanding talent of them both made their closeness easy and natural, and their subsequent friendship solid, sincere and lasting.

When they went on vacation, they wrote to each other, and this need for mutual communication persevered forever. Myaskovsky's brilliant, witty style amazed even Sergei Alexeyevich: "Just to think that somebody can write such letters!" Prokofiev's literary gift was in no way inferior to that of his friend, and, as a result, the volume of the letters of the two musicians is a true treasure of literature.

The subject of the more than four hundred and fifty letters is music. Because of their mutual respect and affection, the two could criticize each other's works sharply and severely, for only absolute, uncompromising honesty makes one a true friend and a true artist. Admiration, too, was expressed generously and joyfully: "It's worth living on earth while such music is composed!" Myaskovsky wrote to Prokofiev in April 1928, in reference to *The Angel of Fire*.

In their student years, they were fond of examining musical novelties together; they were also "addicted" to playing in four hands. And, early in 1908, Prokofiev and Myaskovsky were admitted to the St. Petersburg group, "Soirees of Modern Music."

Enthusiasts of new art gathered on Thursdays to talk and listen to new works; sometimes, they also held public concerts. Their discussions and arguments were "permeated with a spirit of extremely intense artistic search and strict evaluation of the fruits . . ." The "Soirees" were guided by knowledgeable and devoted musicians, such as V. F. Nouvel, A. P. Nurok, critic V. G. Karatygin. It was at these "Modern Music" concerts that works by Dukas, Debussy, Chausson, Ravel, Schoenberg were heard in Russia for the first time. It was at the "Soirees" that the Russian public "discovered" Stravinsky. Myaskovsky and Prokofiev, too, owed their first recitals to this group.

On December 18, 1908, the public of St. Petersburg was, for the first time, invited to hear Sergei Prokofiev's works. The program of the concert in the College Hall featured music by Grieg, Cherepnin, Vitol, Taneyev, and also by beginners: Myaskovsky (three poems by Zinaida Gippius set to music) and Prokofiev (billed as "Piano Pieces"). Mariya Grigorievna and Morolev were in the audience. Prokofiev's powerful mastery of piano techniques stunned the audience. The debutant was rather wary about his success (". . . Now let us listen to the ravings of the critics, of whom I think there were six"), but several days later, there were favorable reviews of his performance in the St. Petersburg newspapers. The most friendly of them (signed "N. Sem.") was printed in the *Slovo* (The Word) of December 20, 1908:

"Throughout the fancies of this rich creative imagination, one perceives an extraordinary and undoubted talent, a talent as yet unbalanced, falling under the power of every impulse; a talent that is taken in by extravagant conjunctions of sounds and skillfully finds a logical basis for the most risky modulations. The pieces vary greatly in mood—now impulsive and stormy ('Despair'), now composedly pensive ('Remembrance'), now fantastic('Snow'); now, they stun by wild play of imagination ('Obsession'). Sincerity, absence of artificiality and intentional search for the harmonically unusual, and a truly outstanding talent are evident in the logical development of thought, form and contents. A great imaginative power and inventiveness supply the author with even more artistic material than he could need."

In that same year, 1908, Prokofiev's music was, for the first time, performed by an orchestra. "S. Prokofiev has come back from his summer vacation with a symphony (in E minor, three movements). It's fresh, and the Andante is quite wonderful," Myaskovsky wrote in his diary. The free and plastic forms of the Andante theme suggest the future Prokofiev with his sweeping, free-breathing melodies. The performance of the symphony depended totally on Glazunov: ". . . through him, one can get to the Royal Orchestra, and the Sheremetev Orchestra, and the Conservatory Orchestra. But to make him do something, one must urge him on constantly, and so I have assaulted him more than fifteen times already . . ." The author's persistence proved to be effective. The Royal Orchestra, conducted by Gugo Varlikh, performed the symphony at a closed rehearsal. As the composer himself remembers, "the impression was dim," even

Claude Debussy.

though Nurok's remark that it was "nice music to doze to," offended him.

Studies in the composition class were about to end. In the last year, Prokofiev began to study with Iosif Ivanovich Vitol, a well-known Lettish composer. Vitol did not show any interest in Prokofiev's innovations; the only good thing was that he did not try to hamper them. The summation he gave of Prokofiev at the finals was quite one-sided: "An innovator to the extreme, with a rather narrowly developed technique." The finals were held in the spring of 1909; it was then that the divergence of the young composer's aspirations from those of his teachers became clear. The Sixth Piano Sonata and the new version of the final scene of the *Feast During The Plague* irritated the examiners, especially Lyadov, who had failed, after all, to curb his self-willed pupil. But Prokofiev received a diploma and the title of "free artist."

Many of his fellow-students were embarking on independent careers in art, not linked to the Conservatory. But Prokofiev decided to continue his education as a pianist. He was excited by the very attractive prospect of studying under Anna Nikolaevna Yessipova, whose class was the "avant-garde of the Conservatory."

His former piano teacher, A. A. Vinkler, had been diligent and systematic. He had managed to get the young man to like playing old gavottes and composing his own; he was one of the first to respond to his best pupil's public debut in the College Hall by writing a serious article for the *St. Petersburger Zeitung* of December 24, 1908. In that article, Vinkler wrote: "Prokofiev is still very young and, as of now, in the *Sturm und Drang* period; he is also strongly influenced by the new decadent trend in art. But, when the process of maturation is completed, one can expect most excellent fruits from his extraordinary talent." His classes, however, were boring and soon were of no more use to Prokofiev, whose technique was developed sufficiently.

It was not without awe that the young man looked forward to transferring to Yessipova's class; even in the summer of 1908, he asked Myaskovsky for advice on choosing the Beethoven sonata to play for Anna Nikolaevna.

The famous pianist, professor of the St. Petersburg Conservatory since 1893, continued to give highly successful concerts. Together with violinist L. Auer, she appeared in sonata evening concerts, more exciting to the music lovers of St. Petersburg than any touring celebrities. Yessipova's performance was quite compelling, with its lofty artistic style and the refined taste of a true artist. Her majestic hands made the piano keys sing, and she taught her pupils to "vary body movements, so that performance came closer to conversation." True, Yessipova did not recognize modern composers, but she took interest in her new pupil's work: ". . . On the side, she used to talk about the kind of students she had now: they write sonatas! (I had given the final touch to my Sonata op. 1 and played it for Yessipova; she took the music home and marked the pedal)." Yet since that spring the eighteen-year-old boy had the title of "free artist" and was as willful as ever.

This page and opposite:
Program of Sergei Prokofiev's first public performance in one of the "Soirees of Modern Music" on December 18, 1908, he playing his own piano pieces.

Yessipova's regard for texts was well-known, and Prokofiev would, without much deliberation, add a note or two to a classic's work, or throw out "unnecessary" ones. Their attitudes toward each other were respectful but cool. Yessipova's statement for the finals was: "He has not fully grasped my method. He is very talented but somewhat rough." Prokofiev later remembered the professor's unwillingness to respect the student's individuality.

Youthful boldness clashed with the indomitable will of the wise, experienced artist yet resulted in a quaint but fruitful alliance. In Yessipova's class, Prokofiev rid himself of the defects in his performance—sloppiness, the habit of playing with sweeping strokes, carelessly. Despite constant arguments and frictions, a future treasure of Russian culture was being molded—the brilliant pianistic mastery of Prokofiev . . .

"You have no ability for conducting, but since I believe in you as a composer and I know you will often have to perform your own works, I shall teach you how to conduct," Nikolai Nikolaevich Cherepnin, who had admitted Prokofiev to his already crowded conducting class, declared at one of the lessons.

The poetic music of Cherepnin's ballets and symphonies glittered with languid modulations of delicate and slightly cold tones. The titles, reminiscent of antiquity—*Armida's Pavillion, Narcissus and Echo, Bacchus*—emphasized the affinity between his aspirations and the trends of the "Mir Iskusstva" impressionism and esthetics. It was Cherepnin who was entrusted with assisting in the Paris production of *The Snow Maiden*; his education and conscientiousness made him reliable. On the other hand, his favorite pupil's obvious inclination to "modernism" made Rimsky-Korsakov wish he could caution him. The comment in Rimsky-Korsakov's Diary on Cherepnin's project to write an opera in a "creative trio," with Meyerhold and Golovin, is brief but significant: "I am trying to persuade him to compose independently, without those two."

Young, energetic, all "woven out of contrast," his slightly prominent eyes quick and sharp, Cherepnin proved to be the only teacher in the Conservatory to support young Prokofiev's aspirations unreservedly. "Even though he composed more eclectically than he spoke of music, and conducted less convincingly than he talked about conducting, yet contact with him was extremely beneficial." Cherepnin captured his interest with a conception of a *Eugene Onegin* that was to be very different from Tchaikovsky's opera, but faithful to Pushkin's book. Of Brahms, he said: ". . . this is absolutely pure music. One cannot take it apart, cog by cog, and then examine each one of them to see if it is beautiful; one must understand that this music is crystal clear, running like a wonderful spring." Prokofiev, later admitting that he was an immature opponent for Cherepnin at that time, remembered their conversations on music with gratitude and affection.

An important outcome of studies with Cherepnin is that Prokofiev acquired not only conducting skills, but a vivid interest in Haydn and Mozart, in the light elegance of old dance tunes. A product of Prokofiev's "classicism" in his Conservatory years was

Well-known pianist Anna
Yessipova was, Prokofiev later
reminisced, "regarded as the best
professor at the Conservatory . . .
If the student's individuality was
compatible with Yessipova's, the
results were marvellous."

Prokofiev's conducting teacher
Nikolai Cherepnin, "a brilliant
musician who could speak with
equal interest and love of old
music and of the most new.
. . .One derived great benefits
from contact with him."

the Symphoniette in A major. The piece has a stylistic "framing" —the gracious classicism of the opening and the conclusion is set off by the fanciful, grotesque images of the Andante and the Scherzo. Prokofiev rewrote the early score twice, in 1914 and in 1929, admitting that his "skills were not good enough for such delicate writing."

While studying under Cherepnin, Prokofiev conducted at student recitals and performances. His interest in the activities of the opera class prompted him to compose a new one-act opera, *Maddalena*, with a thrillingly dramatic plot, an intensity of musical atmosphere, an unbroken line of dynamic intensification toward the bloody finale.

The young composer was drawn to romantic art: Scriabin and Rachmaninov. The influence of their music is felt in Prokofiev's symphonic tableau *Dreams*, and in the sketch *Autumn*. *Dreams* conveys an atmosphere of dusk; the music unfolds somewhat slowly. Prokofiev dedicated this work to Scriabin—"the author who began with *Dreams*." *Autumn* was inspired by Rachmaninov's music of the 1900's—the symphonic poem *The Isle of the Dead* and Symphony No. 2. The gloom and "resignation" of the mood had nothing to do with landscape images. "Critics wrote of drizzling rain and falling leaves, quoted poetry —but none of them realized that it was a picture of the inner, not the outer world, and that this *Autumn* can happen in spring or in summer," he wrote to Myaskovsky.

Along with mastering the symphony orchestra, Prokofiev composed pianoforte music. Even before transferring to Yessipova's class, he wrote six sonatas for his favorite instrument. Myaskovsky remarked cautiously, "You needn't be so keen on putting down numbers for your sonatas. A moment will still come when you will cross it all out and write: Sonata No. 1." And, even though his words soon proved right, Prokofiev did not reject his earlier experiments. The themes of the early sonatas were, so to say, diffused in later piano compositions. Short piano pieces were included in op. 3 and 4. Evolved from childhood "little songs," they suggest the principal imagery of Prokofiev's music— dramatic outbursts, eccentric humor, dreamy lyrical passages. The four etudes of op. 2 are remarkable for their propensity for a strong, romantic piano style. They are linked to the transfer from Vinkler's class to Yessipova's: ". . . I decided to write four technical etudes in summer and dedicate them to him. It will be a memory of the time I spent in his class."

In 1910, the Prokofiev family suffered the death of the father. Now the young man had to take care of himself and his mother. The new situation required energy, activity, willpower— qualities that he possessed fully. A struggle for the recognition of his works began. This was much harder than composing them: musical publishing houses refused to print them, well-known conductors refused to perform them.

"August 9 (22), 1910

"Dear Sir!

"Through our Moscow Department, we mail to you your manu-

Editor-in-chief of the *Muzika* weekly V.V. Derzhanovsky, whom Prokofiev called "a courageous fighter for decent music."

scripts: Sonata op. 1 and two etudes op. 2; we inform you that the board has not found it possible to publish these compositions.

"Very respectfully,
The Musical Publishing House of Russia"

He received many similar letters—from Jurgenson, from Bessel, from the Musical Publishing House of Russia, concert sponsors—even though he tried persistently to find his way to the audience. He turned to Taneyev for help; Myaskovsky defended him passionately: "Oh, were I a musical publisher, I would do anything I could to spare the poor composers all the disgusting humiliations they have to undergo for the sake of commercial profits and for the pleasure of all kinds of puffed-up egos." Slowly and reluctantly, the ice barrier of caution and rejection began to melt.

This was a period of a sort of re-evaluation of tastes in Russian art. What seemed new and unquestionably interesting only a short while ago did not satisfy now. Many musicians, having gone through a stage of ventures in impressionism, began to search for a more meaningful and dynamic art, in contrast to the static beauty and the self-sufficient novelty of form in the works of late followers of Impressionism and Scriabinism.

The weekly *Muzika* (*Music*) magazine played an important part in the movement for new art. Prokofiev's fellow-student, the young critic B. V. Asafiev, wrote passionate, sharply critical articles for the magazine; Myaskovsky published in it a most important landmark of Russian critical thought of that time—his article "Beethoven and Tchaikovsky." The remarkable thing about the article is that it mentions the subject of the national dignity of Russian musicians, of the struggle for independent, sublime art, free of slavish imitations of the West. "With all the fuss they raise about everything that comes from abroad, they turn away, with a truly Russian vandalism, from everything that is our own. This should be eradicated," Myaskovsky wrote in a letter. In Prokofiev, Myaskovsky and Asafiev saw the hope of Russian art; it was in his resolute, lucid creative work that the ideal of future Russian music was to be realized. "It is such a delight, and also such a surprise, to find this bright and healthy phenomenon in the heaps of present-day effeminacy, debility and anaemia," Myaskovsky wrote.

The first to recognize Prokofiev's talent were conductors K. S. Saradzhev and A. P. Aslanov. The Moscow circle of critic V. V. Derzhanovsky and conductor K. S. Saradzhev, connected with the *Muzika* magazine, organized large symphony concerts in the open-air summer music-hall of the Sokolniki park. The sympathetic attitude of the circle's leaders made it possible for Prokofiev to perform his compositions before large audiences.

On July 25, 1912, he performed Piano Concerto No. 1 in the People's House. The premiere was a brilliant success, even though the critics' opinions were split. Karatygin, Derzhanovsky, Myaskovsky were delighted by the new composition. Ill-

V.G. Karatygin.

wishers—and there already were some among the critics—fulminated against the Concerto, denouncing it as "musical filth" and demanding a straitjacket for the author. From now on, every new work of his would be received with an avalanche of articles and reviews; opinions, discussions, would storm about him.

The composition had been first conceived as a piano concertino. The form, expanded "from within," is monolithic, despite the variety of contrasting episodes and the free, rhapsodic style. Quite characteristic are both the vigorous outline of the first subject with its laconic intonations, moving implacably towards the climax, and the "steely" rhythm, cementing the whole composition together. The powerful imperative is heard three times in the Concerto—"the three whales," according to Prokofiev, that form the basis of the composition. In the coda, the exultant tones of the opening theme conclude the sequence of the main part's diverse images.

The ill-wishers' ferocious critique could not discourage Prokofiev. His determination, his firm conviction that the way he had chosen was right, helped him move forward confidently, ignoring the attack of the short-sighted conservatives.

The imperious power of Concerto No. 1, its magnitude and brilliance, immediately placed Prokofiev in the avant-garde ranks of Russia's cultural life. In August 1913, he received his first, long-awaited notice from a reputable concert institution, Sergei Kussevitsky's Concert Management:

"Dear Sir,

"We hereby have the honor to invite you to participate in the 7th concert of the 2nd series of 'Symphony Matinees At Available Prices,' which is to take place on Sunday, February 16, 1914 in Moscow, in the Grand Hall of the Noble Assembly.

"We request you to perform your Piano Concerto."

Success called for new ventures in the genre he came to love. And, shortly after the premiere of Concerto No. 1 in late 1912, Prokofiev wrote another piano concerto. "Charges of external brilliance pursued for its own sake and of some 'football-like' quality in Concerto No. 1 led me to search for greater depth of meaning in No. 2." The intensified work at perfection of piano technique was reflected in the music of his new work: the piano dominates, its part is rich in variety of invention, the texture is complex and even decorative.

The four movements of the Concerto are treated by Prokofiev freely, with no adherence to the generally accepted norm. The dynamic of motion is directed toward the apotheosis of wild, turbulent forces in the finale's ending. The starting point of this progress is the simple, solemn theme of movement 1. In its development, it changes beyond recognition, taking on traits of a grim force of nature. In the middle of the cycle are two unexpectedly fast parts: the scherzo, a whirlwind of solo passages, and the intermezzo, the raging of a grotesque, somewhat sinister fantasy. The same images are dominant in the finale, with its turbulent dramatic tension, its harsh sonorities. ". . . In my opinion, the clarity of form, the concentration of thought, the precision

The first page of the manuscript of Piano Concerto no. 2.

and well-roundedness of expression make this a classic concerto," Myaskovsky wrote, delighted. "When I was reading your concerto this night, lying in bed, I went almost crazy with admiration; I jumped and cried out, so that, if I had neighbors, they would have probably thought I was mad. You're an angel!"

On August 23, 1913 the Concerto was performed by the author in Pavlovsk, directed by Aslanov. The reviewer of the *Peterburgskaya Gazeta* (*The St. Petersburg Gazette*) left a vivid description of this memorable premiere:

"A stripling who looks like a Peterschule student appears on stage. That is S. Prokofiev. He sits down at the piano and begins to do something that looks as if he's either dusting the keys, or trying them out to see which ones sound higher or lower. Then follows a sharp, dry stroke . . . Some are indignant. A couple gets up and makes its way to the exit—such music can drive you crazy! Is he making fun of us or something? . . . Other people in the audience follow the example of that first couple. Prokofiev plays the second movement of his concerto. Again, a rhythmic chaos of sounds. The audience, or at least the boldest part of it, hisses. More and more empty seats. At last, the young artist concludes his recital with a pitilessly discordant combination of the brasses. The audience is quite scandalized. The majority is hissing. Prokofiev bows defiantly and plays an encore."

The city papers heaped an avalanche of abuse on the new composition. It was the lone voice of Karatygin that accurately predicted the future of the composer: "The audience hissed. Well, that's all right. In about ten yers it will redeem yesterday's whistles with unanimous applause for the new famous composer of European renown!"

In the last years of study in the Conservatory, Prokofiev had to divide his time among conducting, composition and classes with Yessipova. New works were usually written in summer. After his father's death, there was no more possibility of privacy in Sontzovka, and new place names appear on the envelopes of his letters to friends in vacation time: Kislovodsk, Sukhum, Yalta, Teriorki, and, in summer 1913, also Paris, London, Geneva.

The pace of his life was as fast as ever. He organized his time very well and spent it gainfully, fruitfully, enjoying it, too. He still played chess. "I was hungry for a strong partner," and this longing brought him to the dimly lit tables of the solemn, austere hall of the Chess Society on the Nevsky Avenue. As a musician he enjoyed chess, finding in it the intensity of temperamental duel, the beauty of a composition shaped with inspiration, a composition with relatively peaceful moments followed by sudden outbursts, with periods of gradually increasing hidden tension breaking out suddenly in dramatic combinations.

He played chess with relatives and friends, by correspondence, in one-time game sessions; he read literature on chess, became acquainted with champions. When Emmanuel Lasker arrived for a chess tournament, Prokofiev rushed to the train station to meet him, enlisted hurriedly for a one-time game session and ended the game with the chessmaster in a draw. A few years later, he

The concert stage in Pavlovsk. Engraving on wood by Ostroumova-Lebedeva.

K.S. Saradzhev, an early
enthusiastic admirer of Sergei
Prokofiev who conducted the
premiere of his Piano Concerto no. 1.

London.

was even lucky enough to win a game with Capablanca. He also wrote an article for the newspaper *Dyen* (*Day*) about the game between the two great chess-players, with witty parallels from the world of music.

"It was with great excitement that I followed the wonderful contest which took place on the premises of the Chess Society. Capablanca's brilliant style, the easy and gracious way in which he defeated his opponents drew all the sympathy to him in the very first days. But Lasker, after all, was so consistent, so uncompromising, so intelligent in the way he played that one simply couldn't help bowing to the Chess King. I would like to compare these two pillars of the chess world to two geniuses of the music world, Mozart and Bach. And, while I see the complex, deep Lasker as the majestic Bach, the lively and impetuous Capablanca is the eternally young Mozart who created with the same ease, and sometimes the same dear carelessness, as Capablanca.

"In addition to this, a little compliment for Dr. Tarrash. I happened to hear him play the piano, and it was a pleasure. The precision of rhythm, the clarity of phrasing and the general expressiveness speak for the famous chessmaster's great musical gift.

"Sergei Prokofiev
May 9, 1913"

In the spring of 1914, Prokofiev graduated from the Conservatory with a triumph. The best student, Cherepnin's pride, he earned an "excellent" grade at the conducting exam. Besides, the self-conscious graduate was excited by the competitive atmosphere that prevailed in the piano classes. "I became prey to ambition and decided to graduate at the top of the class." Yessipova was seriously ill; there was no hope of her returning to teach. It was left to himself to prepare for the finals and make up the program. As his larger form composition, he decided to present his Piano Concerto No. 1. The Conservatory administration consented, though reluctantly, but demanded that each examiner should have the opportunity to have a look at the piano score of the new composition in advance. The young man pressed Jurgenson to hurry with the publication of the Concerto, for "delay can get me into serious trouble, up to being barred from the finals." The publishing house met the deadline, and when Prokofiev came forth to the piano, he saw members of the jury open twenty brand new copies of the Concerto score.

The virtuoso power and mastery of his piano style stunned the examiners. Despite a long, heated argument, despite the protests of a group of influential professors, including Glazunov, Prokofiev was recognized as the winner. For many years, he kept the receipt for a Schroeder piano (such was the A. G. Rubinstein prize) and a newspaper clipping, "The Conservatory Laureate," with a picture of a young man with a fashionable hairstyle, wearing a bright-colored striped tie. He was interviewed, his talent was recognized even by those who only a short while ago refused to consider him a musician. His final exam will remain in the history of the Conservatory as the triumph of an already mature

Sergei Prokofiev in the graduating Conservatory class of 1914.

artist. And, for all the irreconcilable controversy his disturbing, fiery temperament raised, he will be able to confront all criticism with the firm conviction of an artist forging the cast forms of his compositions at the piano.

The prize piano Prokofiev received as the top student in his graduating class.

Prokofiev. A 1918 drawing by
Alexander Benoît.

After Graduation

After his brilliantly successful graduation from the Conservatory in the spring of 1914, in the piano and conducting classes, Prokofiev's name became extremely popular in the music world. He was invited to participate in concerts; large publishing houses printed his works, accepting the conditions he laid down.

In the summer of 1914, Prokofiev received a gift from his mother – permission to travel to London. The trip turned out to be quite eventful. The young musician met Shalyapin and conductor Pierre Monteux, attended a performance of Richard Strauss (and found the music of the ballet *The Legend of Joseph* "ridiculously meaningless"). In London, he made an acquaintance that, to a great extent, determined Prokofiev's future artistic career: V. F. Nouvel introduced him to Dyaghilev.

Sergei Pavlovich Dyaghilev is one of the most original figures in Russian artistic culture. At the turn of the century he was co-founder, with Alexandre Benoît, of the "Mir Iskusstva" ("World of Art") artistic community; he served in the administration of royal theatres, organized art exhibitions. After the 1904 revolution, at the time when every new thought in the public and cultural life of Russia was stifled by the wave of reaction, Dyaghilev went to the West more and more often, to bring Russian art to Europe. "He adored Russia and all things Russian with a fanatical zeal; rarely has there been a man of such patriotic pride," A. Benoît wrote. Dyaghilev displayed Russian works abroad as examples of an original, youthful creative art which could and should ". . . be a new word in European art".

In the fall of 1906, in twelve halls of "The Fall Salon," Parisians viewed the "Two Centuries of Russian Painting and Sculpture" exhibition, with Russian music sounding at the display of pictures. The next season was devoted to organizing symphony concerts of the works of Russian composers, from Glinka to Rachmaninov and Scriabin, in Paris. In 1908, *Boris Godunov* with Shalyapin in the leading part, was produced for the first time on the Grand Opera stage.

The sophisticated habitués of Paris theatres were stunned by the magnificent stage sets in the coronation scene, as well as by the acting and singing mastery of the chorus. For the first time in the history of Parisian opera, the chorus got an ovation, and,

Cartoon sketch of Richard Strauss conducting *Salome*.

"I am convinced that we are living in a frightful era of crisis; we are to die, so that a new culture can come forth and take over that which will be left of our tired wisdom."

Sergei Dyaghilev

World-famous Russian bass Fyodor Shalyapin as Boris Godunov.

after the first scene of the Prologue, the curtain rose and fell several times. Shalyapin's powerful bass soared upward in the Grand Opera hall, and the eyes of the audience were riveted on the stage. And there he was, pacing majestically, dashing around wildly, stopping suddenly, as if rooted to the ground by the terror of evil forebodings — Tsar Boris, intelligent yet weak-willed, full of noble intentions yet criminal . . .

Since 1909, after Mikhail Fokin's production of *The Polovetzian Dances* from Borodin's *Prince Igor*, Dyaghilev's activity was centered on ballet. The impresario organized his own ballet company (called "Sergei Dyaghilev's Russian Ballet" since 1913) and toured Europe and America with it.

Dyaghilev managed to gather a remarkable creative body. A. Benoît, L. Bakst, N. Roerich, P. Picasso designed stage sets for his productions. Music by Debussy, Ravel, Richard Strauss, Satie was used in the performances. Anna Pavlova, Tamara Karsavina, Vaslav and Bronislava Nijinsky danced. Aspiring to create a new national ballet, the company's managers turned to the young composers they regarded as the hope of Russian music, Stravinsky and Prokofiev.

Every production was born in arguments and conflicts among outstanding masters, led by Dyaghilev's will and hand of steel. His fine taste and unimpeachable intuition enabled him to perceive unerringly what the audience wanted and to anticipate the changes. The spirit of ardor and polemics that pervaded his day-to-day work was also visible in everything Dyaghilev wrote for the press.

The impresario's work was quite controversial. He was infinitely devoted to Russian art — yet, while working at the development of national ballet, he was virtually torn from Russian life and reality. The fast evolution of Dyaghilev's tastes, his constant desire to be "at the crest of the wave," to dictate trends in art, often resulted in aimless eccentricity, especially in later productions. All his activities were carried on under the guise of material disinterestedness, yet he always had to reckon with those who aided him with grants. After Prokofiev interrupted the orchestra at the dress rehearsal of *The Clown,* Dyaghilev came up to him and "whispered, his face distorted, 'I have brought the cream of London society to your rehearsal, and you spoiled the whole thing with your interruption. Please, no more interruptions, whatever happens.' "

"He was an aristocrat who knew his own value, who looked austere, chic, smart and elegant in his irreproachable Sunday clothes," Asafiev reminisced. The personality of Dyaghilev, infinitely devoted to his cause and extremely egotistical at the same time, left no one indifferent. Temperamental, excitable, he knew how to establish his authority over people and make them do what he demanded. Artists of high individuality and strong will worked with Sergei Pavlovich willingly and with inspiration, creating their very best. Prokofiev's rebellious genius surrendered with enthusiasm to the power of his spell.

Dyaghilev tried to bring Prokofiev as close to his company as

Igor Stravinsky with great dancer Nijinsky in the costume of Petrushka.

he could. And so, every evening a seat was reserved for Prokofiev at performances of the "Russian Ballet," and at intermissions and after the performances, the composer immersed himself in the beautiful, half-real world behind the scene.

A circle of choreographers, artists, close friends heard Piano Sonata No. 2, Concerto No. 2 and *Maddalena*. "I tried to shift the attention to the opera and to *The Gambler*, but failed," the composer wrote to Myaskovsky. The company needed a choreographic work, and a ballet "on a Russian folk-tale or prehistoric subject" was conceived. "The last thing Dyaghilev said to me was that he wished, by all means, to have my ballet by the next season," and Prokofiev set to work together with the young poet Sergei Gorodetzky.

At that time, the beginning of World War I brought sudden changes into Russian life. Chauvinistic appeals and bombastic, false patriotism cannot fool or lure anyone capable of thinking. The monstrous, bloody slaughter at the front created a mood of gloomy, hopeless apathy among all those who had looked into the horrifying face of the war, at that time the worst humanity had gone through.

Myaskovsky was at the front, sharing hunger, misery and military dangers with the soldiers. Prokofiev, who had been allowed to remain in St. Petersburg as "a widowed mother's only son," read the letters of his friend, full of impressions of life in the trenches, and replied in an almost apologetic tone: ". . . It's even embarrassing to write to you about our peaceful trifling affairs."

The "peaceful trifling affairs" Sergei Sergeievich referred to was work at the ballet *Ala and Lolliy* for Dyaghilev. For a libretto, Gorodetzky offered an Ancient Slavic mythical subject based on his own early collection of poetry, *Yar* (Ancient Slavic for "Light"). Images of Ancient Russia, of Scythians, and an Ancient Slavic sun-worshipping cult were being created in those years by Russian artists (N. Roerich), writers (A. Blok), musicians (I. Stravinsky). Concentrated, sometimes high-strung expression and exquisitely complex form were strangely and organically combined in their works with primitive roughness—like a fiery whirlpool of reality reflected in the age-polished surface of a wooden idol with its impassive but captivating look.

Prokofiev, immersed in his work, tirelessly invented the most unheard of, the most barbaric and frightening dissonances and timbre effects. In early February 1915 he joined Dyaghilev in Italy, with the piano score of the fully completed ballet.

The great impresario was not easy to please. He received Prokofiev warmly but rejected both the libretto and the music, finding the script uninteresting and the music not original enough ("It's no more than music in general . . ."). But his interest in Prokofiev's talent proved to be firm and solid. Dyaghilev wrote to Stravinsky: "I'll bring him to you. He must change entirely. Otherwise, we're going to lose him forever . . ."

Striving to capture and hold Prokofiev's interest, Dyaghilev introduced him to the charms of Italy—the treasury of culture, the land of museums, of age-old ruins and beautiful nature. He arranged for

Drawing of Igor Stravinsky by Marc Chagall.

**Prokofiev vacationing in Pavlovsk,
in 1915.**

Outstanding Russian ballerina Tamara Karsavina as Colombine in Stravinsky's *Petrushka*.

a recital for Prokofiev and in the evening of March 7, Piano Concerto No. 2 was heard in the Augusteum Hall in Rome.

The young composer admired Italian landscapes, but the music of Italian futurists left him cold and indifferent. His article "The Futurists' Musical Instruments," written for *Muzika* magazine, was very cool, quite unlike his usual fiery statements in the press.

The company's goal was to create new shows based on Russian subjects. Young Stravinsky's "Dyaghilev" works (*The Firebird, Petrushka, The Rite of Spring*) were among the first Russian ballets with Russian-based librettos. A synthesis of Dyaghilev's aspirations and Prokofiev's interest in folklore gave birth to the idea of the next ballet, *The Clown*, based on Russian folk tales from Afanasiev's collection. Having signed his first real contract, the composer went back to St. Petersburg.

At home, Prokofiev began to give recitals on a large scale. His contact with Dyaghilev made him even more famous. The Russian Musical Society opened its doors to the young musician; previously, its concerts were available to "orthodox academicians" only. The performance of Prokofiev's compositions caused much comment in the press.

At that time, Prokofiev worked at two larger compositions, *The Clown* and *The Scythian Suite*, born of the music for the ballet *Ala and Lolliy*, rejected by Dyaghilev.

The premiere of *The Scythian Suite* on January 16, 1916 was the worst scandal in the history of all the premières of Prokofiev's works. Most of the audience was indignant, and Glazunov "lost his patience and left the hall, unable to bear the sunrise—that is, eight minutes before the end." Reviewers poured out a torrent of scathing criticism, calling the suite "a waste of music paper." But the stormy reception of the performance did not upset Prokofiev, and on the next day he wrote to Moscow quite serenely, "Yesterday, I conducted *Ala*, which created a great lot of noise."

Even today, one is stunned by the sonorous power of the music, by the simplicity of images that seem hewn out of stone, by the inventiveness of the total construction. The great expressive power of the *Scythian Suite* is in the brilliantly forceful orchestration, in the energy of impetuous rhythms.

Even in the first part, "The Worship of Veles and Ala," the listener is thrown into a gulf of wild, shrill dissonances. In their roar, one can hear savage yells, ominous incantations, the clatter of horses' hooves. Later, the tender, languorous image of the goddess Ala appears, and the sonorous atmosphere changes beyond recognition. To present the threatening, frightful images of part 2 ("Chuzhbog (the alien god) and The Dance Of The Dark Forces"), the composer has found simple but impressive means: stern rhythms, the sharp sounds of eight French horns and four trombones. "Night" is the third part of the score. The fineness, the almost impressionistic picturesqueness of the orchestration are quite impressive. This poetic nocturne is like an islet of calm in the midst of the violent uproar. "Lolliy's Crusade

Manuscript of the literary programme for *The Scythian Suite*.

And The Triumph Of The Sun" is the powerful finale. It presents an act of great retribution: the evil and terrible Chuzhbog is destroyed by the blinding rays of the Sun.

> And, drunk at the feast of triumph,
> Throwing ray after ray of light,
> God Perun lords over the world,
> In his luminous warlike might.

In these brilliant, sonorous passages the finale progresses powerfully towards the radiant "Sunrise."

The sound effects and the exoticism of the *Scythian Suite* did not prevent the most thoughtful of the poet's contemporaries from seeing its willful purposefulness, its life-giving progressive force. Asafiev later wrote: "Prokofiev's music, revealing to us a free will's endeavor towards creative maturity, is profoundly modern, for the whole country now is longing for an active life, for real work, and believes in a radiant future . . . For the destiny of people depends on what they do with it!"

Another manifestation of trends characteristic of the time was a small cycle of five piano pieces entitled, *Sarcasms*. Scepticism, bitter mockery, disappointment, hidden under a mask of mirth, were, according to Asafiev, a reflection of "life's darker forces, its evil, its poison." The climax of the cycle, the highest expression of its tragic spirit was the fifth "Sarcasm," with the author's foreword: "Sometimes, we sneer at somebody or something, but when we look closer, we see how miserable and unhappy what we are mocking at really is; then we feel not quite at ease, laughter sounds in our ears, but now it's a sneer at ourselves . . ."

The opera *The Gambler* was one of the principal works of the pre-revolutionary period, rich in creative achievement. Prokofiev worked at this composition despite the widespread opinion that opera was an obsolete, disappearing genre. The young composer defiantly challenged his authoritative opponents: "Even the most progressive musicians have begun to see operatic form as disappearing. However, with an understanding of the stage, with flexibility, freedom and expressiveness of recitation, opera should be the most original and powerful of all scenic arts."

The piano score of the four-act opera was composed in five and a half months. The composer was in a hurry: the administration of the Marinsky theater was planning for a premiere in 1916.

Prokofiev's fiery temperament, his gift for sarcasm, the power of his satire were embodied in this composition. The "evil and poison" of life, base instincts driving people are concentrated by the composer in characters of condensed expressiveness and almost caricature-like representation. He was attracted by the militant criticism, the accuracy of psychological sketches, the brilliance of prose speech in Dostoyevsky's novel. The heroes of *The Gambler* are crippled by their greed for material wealth; they have no power over themselves; they are wretched in their moral degradation. The power of money corrupts even people of high and noble intent, turns them into Gamblers waiting greedily for the hour of their luck at the table covered with green cloth.

Prokofiev wrote the laconic, eventful libretto himself, preserv-

One of F. Koening's sketches of characters form *The Gambler*.

ing many pages of the novel intact. (It was only for the scene before the last that he turned for help to the writer B. N. Demchinsky). There are several story lines, tightly knit together and, at climactic moments, erupting in a sinister blaze of conflict. "I think the custom of writing opera librettos in verse is a totally absurd conventionality. In this case, Dostoyevsky's prose is more colorful, more multi-dimensional, more convincing than any verse," Prokofiev affirmed.

The vocal declamation of the musical drama *The Gambler*, flexible and precise, frightened many stage producers at that time, but excited Vsevolod Emilievich Meyerhold and made him a devoted admirer of Prokofiev. Meyerhold always strove for a close union of music and conversation in a performance. He supported one of Prokofiev's later ideas with great enthusiasm: "To write an opera for a drama theatre—such an opera that a very musical dramatic actor could deliver his lines against the orchestra background he, Prokofiev, provides, but so that the audience doesn't notice the words are being sung . . ." (Meyerhold told about it in 1929, at a meeting of the Bolshoi Theatre administration). And in the lines of the hero of *The Gambler*, the producer found speech set to music, the "free recitative that requires a dramatic actor."

Prokofiev resting in the country.

. . . In the imaginary town of Roulettenburg a small group of people closely linked to each other is set against the background of the idle society of gamblers. Among them are Alexey, a nervous, defiant seeker of justice, and Polina, who suffers in this atmosphere of money-worship. Polina's stepfather, the General, is also there, waiting impatiently for the death of a rich grandmother in Moscow. Pompous and arrogant, he becomes miserable and servile when he cringingly asks the rich Marquess for money. Charming Blanche, too, is waiting for the multimillionaire inheritance—she is willing to marry the middle-aged General, but not before the respectability of the marriage is confirmed by those millions from Russia.

All hopes for Granny's prompt death are dashed. Formidable and domineering, she appears in Roulettenburg, leaving the General with no prospect of becoming rich. The intrusion of the straightforward, rash Granny not only alters the course of events but also brings contrasting intonations into the music of the opera. Unlike the parts of the other characters, fractured and sharp in patterns, the broad melodics of her speech draw on the intonations of Russian folk songs.

In Act III, the tension grows. Granny, having tasted the delights of gambling, leaves a tremendous amount of money in a casino and goes back to Moscow.

The climactic Act IV is centered around the unforgettable scene of the roulette game. To get money for Polina and thus protect her honor, Alexey goes to a casino. The stage is crowded with actors: gamblers, croupiers, watchers. "A chorus is not flexible or scenic," Prokofiev stated in those years. Therefore, there is no monolithic chorus mass in the roulette scene, but instead, a living, mobile, diverse group of people. Each one has a character and a life of his own and, consequently, a unique musical characteristic. The gamblers' voices are united in a complex, intense ensemble. Alexey gambles, going from table to table, drunk with excitement, forgetting all about Polina. He breaks the bank and rushes back to his hotel, the gamblers' excited remarks drumming ceaselessly in his ears: "He's won two hundred thousand!"

The final dialogue of Alexey and Polina is rich in sharp, almost hysterical intonations. Polina leaves the hero, but that is not Alexey's only tragedy. In his delirium, he remembers the casino, the rolling ball of the roulette, those who were around him in his mad chase for luck and gold. "It was a red twenty times in a row!" the hero cries out in a frenzy, doomed to be a miserable slave of the insatiable roulette . . .

Thus, with bitter and skeptical foresight, ends *The Gambler*, one of Prokofiev's most colorful and original pre-revolutionary works. But Prokofiev's creative aspirations of that period were not limited to the "barbaric" exoticism of the *Scythian Suite* or the morbid grotesque sarcasm of *The Gambler*; there always was a note of lyricism in his music. It was not always heard by contemporaries, and this distressed the young composer. He tells in his *Autobiography* that as early as the summer of 1907 he played to Morolev, one of his most respected friends, the "low-key" finale of the *Ondine*. "I thought it was good to end a long five-act opera with a simple lyrical phrase, without any pomposity. But Morolev did not appreciate my idea. 'It's rather watery,' he pronounced. 'Anyway, how can you conclude a large five-act opera with two soft chords, without a real cadence!'

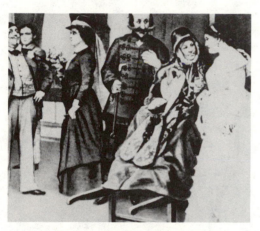

A scene from *The Gambler* at the Theatre de la Monnaie in Brussels, Belgium.

"I sulked. It was hardly possible to prove logically that, on the contrary, it was quite interesting, even touching, for an opera to end in such a way; so I just sulked passively. I had often been reproached with not being lyrical enough; and now, when I had composed a lyrical finale for an opera, nobody appreciated or accepted it. It was annoying, in a word."

Sometimes, friends would offer "lyrical" subjects abundantly seasoned with erotica, but he rejected them as "half-decent mishmash." Prokofiev's delightful lyricism—soft, palpitating, chaste—was blossoming in his music, shy and unnoticed, concentrated in those years in chamber genres.

In the winter of 1915, the composer wrote to V. Derzhanovsky about a "huge, 15-page song based on Andersen's tale, 'The Ugly Duckling.'" The good-hearted, humanistic tale was interpreted by Prokofiev with remarkable warmth and authenticity. The composer loved this work of his. He allotted the song a separate opus: "Let *The Duckling* waddle solo, lest attention should be distracted from it."

That fall, he also set to music five poems by Anna Akhmatova; the genuine humaneness of the songs, with their contrasts of sunny, radiant moods and motives of sadness and despair, is moving. To the delicate, sincere, austere lyrics of the poetess, Prokofiev responded with poetic, hearty music. The melodious *Akhmatova songs* were received with admiration by Myaskovsky, Asafiev, Engel.

At that time, lyrical images also enriched his piano music.

"In every passing moment, many, many worlds I see,
Worlds full of play so changeful, so luminous and free."

These lines of Balmont's poem suggested to Prokofiev the name for a cycle of piano pieces, *Passing Moments*. A motley dance of diverse pictures-images is presented with aphoristic brevity, simply and inventively. Some of the passing moments are restlessly dramatic, fantastic; some are light and full of mirth. In this fanciful work, the first, second, eighth, twelfth, seventeenth and twentieth pieces are remarkably simple and soft. Myaskovsky wrote: "In 'Passing Moments,' one feels an organic expansion, enrichment of the author's soul; one feels that the composer has gone through the phase of an impetuous, headlong run and now begins to stop for a moment, to look around and notice that the universe manifests itself not only in smashing whirlwinds but also, with its continuous movement, in moments of deep peace and quiet pervading the soul . . ."

"For a long time, they denied me lyricism altogether and, unencouraged, it developed slowly," the composer wrote. But, sometimes obscured by the diversity of consonances, by the avalanches of roaring passages, the lyrical motive with its true, subdued beauty sounds more and more confident and bright in his music.

Prokofiev spent the summer of 1916, a year of war, in Finland; from there, he observed the events going on at the front. At the same time, he worked intensively on *The Gambler*. The instrumentation of the opera developed at a truly fantastic speed: eighteen pages of scores a day. The beginning of the last concert season in pre-revolutionary Russia was quite active, too. The young musician performed not only in the capital, but in provinces as well—in Kiev and Saratov. Prokofiev's recitals still provoked critics to cross swords in their fierce discussions of the work of a most original composer of the century.

It was in the pre-revolutionary period that Prokofiev met two great bards of the Russian revolution, Gorky and Mayakovsky.

Since they first met at a literary-musical soirée in February 1917, Alexey Maksimovich (Gorky) held the young composer's talent in high esteem and later, he always took an interest in the development of his work and life. "We're not rich enough to sole soldiers' boots with nails of gold," Gorky remarked as he interceded with the Kerensky government to have Prokofiev exempted from military service.

Mayakovsky was happily excited about the composer's art. "I am now receptive to Prokofiev's music only—the first sounds come, and—life bursts in, no artistic form, but life—a stream rolling downhill, or such a torrent of rain that you run out to have it pour all over you, and shout, oh, how good! More, more!" These well-known words which he said to Asafiev in the summer of 1917 express an admiration of Prokofiev's music, a perception of its surprising affinity to the times. Due to poet Vassily Kaminsky's reminiscences, one of Prokofiev's encounters with Mayakovsky in the Moscow "Cafe of Poets" where, on March 22, 1918, the young composer performed his works, including

Manuscript of the first page of *The Gambler*.

A manuscript of *The Obsession*.

the famous "Obsession," became widely known. "It seemed as if there were a fire in the cafe, and beams and doorposts were falling, in flames like the composer's hair, and we were standing there, ready to burn alive in the fire of this unheard-of music."

Prokofiev was enthusiastic about the February revolution. He saw it as an outburst of tremendous primeval powers, the masses' unprecedented energy. "I greeted it joyously, and so did my milieu. While the revolution was taking place, I was in the streets of St. Petersburg, sometimes hiding behind corners of buildings when the shooting was too hot. The nineteenth *Passing Moment*, written around that time, partly reflects my impressions—the excitement of the crowd rather than the inner substance of the revolution." His strongest impressions of the revolutionary events were also expressed in the cantata *They Are Seven*, and, many years later, the composer brought them back in the music of the Cantata for the twentieth anniversary of the October Revolution.

About the birth of *They Are Seven*, a Chaldean incantation for tenor, mixed chorus and a orchestra, Prokofiev wrote: "The revolutionary events that shook Russia penetrated my soul subconsciously and demanded expression. I did not know how to do it, and, in a strange turn, my imagination flew to the subjects of antiquity. The fact that the thoughts and feelings of that time have survived for millenia stunned me." Prokofiev worked on this composition quickly, with rapture and enthusiasm. "These *Seven* are coming out remarkably well," he wrote. And later, the rebellious offspring of the stormy 1917 remained one of his favorite compositions.

They Are Seven is based on Balmont's poem, "The Accadian Inscription." It speaks of seven formidable giants who rule the world, casting peoples into an abyss of disasters. In a surprising way, the music combines a primeval freedom of temperamental narrative and a precision of logical construction, moments of dynamic tension and periods of rarefaction. The sound effects of the cantata are striking: booming outbursts of the enormous orchestra, archaic psalmody, whisper, glissando in the solo and chorus parts. With all the fiery temperament of his talent, Prokofiev successfully reflected the atmosphere of the exciting era of revolutionary storms in *They Are Seven*.

Even in his youth, the composer was able to work simultaneously on compositions that were amazingly different in content and style. Thus, beside the grandiose sonorities of *They Are Seven* and *The Scythian Suite* the gracious shapes of Symphony No. 1 appear. ". . . Had Haydn lived to our days, he would have retained the manner of his writing, and yet been receptive to some of the new things. That is the kind of symphony I wanted to compose: a symphony classical in style." In the symphony, interest and taste for classical music was combined with Prokofiev's lively humor, his love of wit and jest. Next to *The Scythian Suite* and *They Are Seven*, the gracious score of "The Classical" is like passing from the world of grand orchestral sonorities to a realm of harmony and transparency.

The originality of the 25-year-old composer's individual style is

The cover of Alexander Blok's poem *The Twelve*, which, like Prokofiev's music of that time, reflected the turmoil of the revolutionary era.

Poet Vladimir Mayakovsky.

obvious from the very first notes of the symphony. The mirthful Allegro (movement one) flies by all in one breath, in an impetuous whirlwind. The modal-harmonic shifts brightening the simple, Haydn-like symmetrical melodies are light, easy, playful. The second movement is a tribute to the elegant grace of antique minuets. The ritual of the refined dance is performed with strict observation of the rules, but not without a tinge of mockery: the young jokester catches mirthfully every bow, every curtsey of the affected, slightly straightlaced dancers. The charm of the famous Gavotte (movement three) is in its combination of a generally unpretentious melody and its unexpected momentary twists, of the banality of triadic chords in the shifts and the sharpness of their tonal coordination. Little gems of Prokofiev's wit are liberally scattered throughout the glittering music of the finale—"elementary," painstakingly emphasized *bassi Albertini*, sharp accents, humorous scalar runs. And the conclusion of the motley merry-go-round of shapes is very much like a gesture of Prokofiev the conductor—slightly angular and very resolute.

Prokofiev spent the summer of 1917 in the country, near Petrograd, finishing the Violin Concerto and the Classical Symphony; he read and wrote much. In July, when the city was in danger of occupation by German troops, the composer left for Yessentuki, where his ailing mother was being treated, and then went to Kislovodsk. In a most serene environment, he completed several compositions; sometimes he gave recitals of his own works; he met with Shalyapin and talked with him about "future developments of the opera." As time passed, isolation from life began to oppress both mother and son. "It is sad for me to give in to the hard circumstances and stay here as a refugee, so far from everything I have loved and been used to," Mariya Grigorievna complained in a letter. All attempts to go back failed. And, when the Kaledin rebellion started on the Don, Kislovodsk was entirely cut off from the rest of Russia. It was only nine months later, upon receipt of a protective charter from the Soviet of Worker's Deputies of Kislovodsk, that Prokofiev was able to go to Moscow, and then to Petrograd.

The city was breathing revolution. In spite of the hardships of the first months of their new life, the Petrogradians' enthusiasm for music was as great as ever. Prokofiev gave three recitals of his works. His latest compositions, Sonatas No. 3 and 4 and *Passing Moments*, were performed at two piano soirees, and at a symphony concert the composer first introduced the audience to the Classical Symphony. The premiere was attended by People's Commissar of Education Anatoly Vassilievich Lunacharsky, and several days later he issued a permit to Prokofiev to travel abroad.

"We're all revolutionaries, you in music, we in life, so we've got to work together," Lunacharsky told Prokofiev. During all the time that the composer was abroad, his thoughts always went back to his homeland. His articles appeared in the Soviet press, his compositions were performed at concerts in his country. Musicians, friends, the public followed Prokofiev's achievements with unwavering attention.

"Drama." One of a series of drawings by A.M. Rodchenko illustrating Prokofiev's *Passing Moments*.

Like most artists, young Prokofiev worked in the pre-October period, influenced by a great stimulus—the coming revolution. Its turbulence generated an unprecedented upsurge of the musician's creative energy. An unquenchable youthful force that welcomed the future broke out in him. His music embodies not only a primeval rebellion of denial, but also an appeal to the eternal, simple, and therefore true values of life—love, compassion, goodness.

His contemporaries were amazed by the sharpness and astringency of the language of his music, the capricious movements of his melodics and the unrestrained impetuosity of cheerful, "tonalizing" rhythms. Intense chromaticisms, hard sonorous superimpositions, chords generously seasoned with "stuck-in," non-homogeneous tones. And yet, even in the "Sturm und Drang" period, even in his most daring creations, the pupil of Rimsky-Korsakov and Lyadov, firmly linked with the classical traditions, always achieves clarity and harmony.

The richness of the world of his music is stunning, and Asafiev wrote about it in his article "Roads Into The Future."

"He is primeval and cruel when he comes in touch with outbursts of the animal element in human nature, with its unrestrained sensuality and unconscious rush to the life-giving, all-generating power of the sun. He is inspiredly concentrated when he is striving to comprehend impressions of the phenomena of the inner and outer world that have moved his imagination . . . naive when he tries to depict the struggle of passions; he is pathetically romantic when he speaks of the austere elements of nature or of the charm of old legends; and he is irresistible in his lovely, diary-like moods. He knows laughter—young and playful, or sneering and cold. He also knows the temptation of spells; then, in a sinister half-dark, he is haunted by goblins and distorted reflections of life in the devilish mirror of Andersen's *Snow Queen*! But in all his works, at all times, Sergei Prokofiev is a thoughtful, contemplative artist, and his musical conceptions are never bound by schemes of program or form."

Never had Prokofiev gone through a period so contradictory or been influenced by impressions and acquaintances so different. Unfortunately, his contacts with the great Russian artists who were closely allied with the coming revolution were episodic and could not hasten the process of the musician's civic maturation.

He had never known the humiliations of poverty or social inequality; he had never experienced hopelessness and despair. Throughout his life, he had been composing, performing, worrying about the future of his new works. He had never seen blood and death at the front and had no idea of the new life his country was entering. Jealously guarding his independence, he was growing alienated from reality. A true son of his epoch, he greeted the great renewal in his art; an intellectual isolated from social perturbations, he could not understand the October events when they happened.

He had to go through the temptations and disillusionments, the successes and failures of many years of travelling in order to achieve full maturity as artist and citizen.

Petrograd in 1917.

Writer Maxim Gorky.

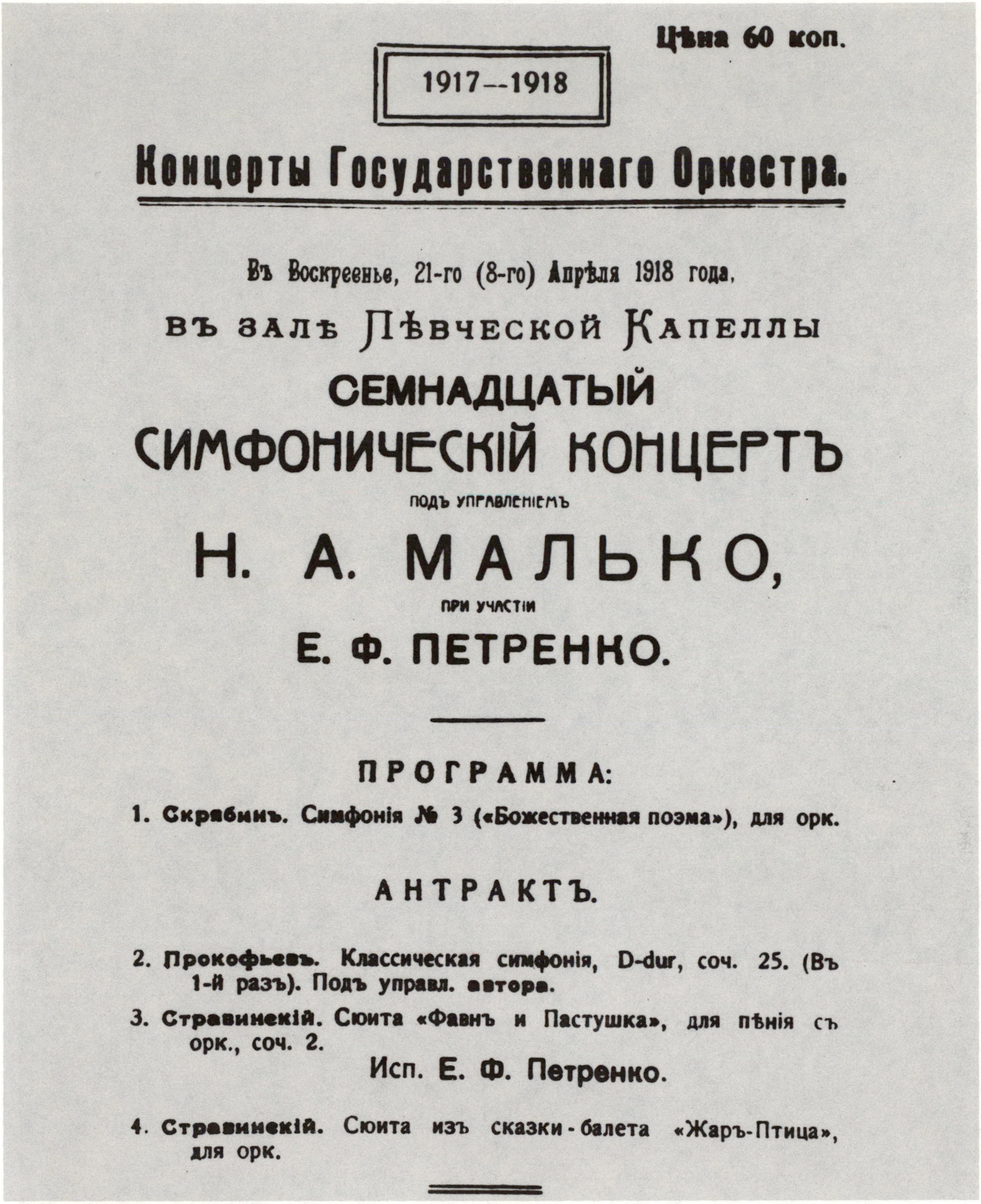

1917—1918

Концерты Государственнаго Оркестра.

Въ Воскресенье, 21-го (8-го) Апрѣля 1918 года,

въ залѣ Пѣвческой Капеллы

СЕМНАДЦАТЫЙ
СИМФОНИЧЕСКIЙ КОНЦЕРТЪ

ПОДЪ УПРАВЛЕНIЕМЪ

Н. А. МАЛЬКО,

ПРИ УЧАСТIИ

Е. Ф. ПЕТРЕНКО.

ПРОГРАММА:

1. **Скрябинъ.** Симфонiя № 3 («Божественная поэма»), для орк.

АНТРАКТЪ.

2. **Прокофьевъ.** Классическая симфонiя, D-dur, соч. 25. (Въ 1-й разъ). Подъ управл. автора.

3. **Стравинскiй.** Сюита «Фавнъ и Пастушка», для пѣнiя съ орк., соч. 2.

   Исп. Е. Ф. Петренко.

4. **Стравинскiй.** Сюита изъ сказки-балета «Жаръ-Птица», для орк.

Program of the concert in which
Prokofiev's Classical Symphony
(second piece on the program) was
premiered.

Prokofiev in the early 1920s.

The Years of Travelling

It took a long time to get to the New World. Eighteen days on the Transsiberian Express to Vladivostok, two months of forced stay in Japan, and, finally, a long voyage by sea to San Francisco, via Honolulu. America received Prokofiev with curiosity and skepticism. His very first concerts made it clear that American audiences did not accept his lyricism but applauded "the volcanic eruptions at the keyboard," scarcely recognized his talent as a composer but were enthusiastic about his piano technique, especially when popular compositions by Rachmaninov and Scriabin were included in the program. Just as in Russia, his performances received mixed and sensational reviews. Newspapers vied with each other:

"... When the dinosaur's daughter was graduating from the Conservatory of that time, she had Prokofiev in her repertoire ..."

"... He is one of the most remarkable pianists and one of the most exciting composers to have emerged from that country of endless trouble ..."

"... Steel fingers, steel wrists, steel biceps, steel triceps ... It's a steel thrust of sound ..."

In some reviews, Prokofiev's music was branded "Bolshevist," while other audiences saw him as a messenger of the Revolution. "He is a revolutionary artist. Workers must listen to his music. He breathes freedom," a Chicago workers' paper said.

Prokofiev had taken with him from Russia a copy of the theatrical magazine published by Vsevolod Meyerhold and a group of people active in the new Russian theatre. The magazine was named after the play, based on Carlo Gozzi's tale, that appeared in the first issue—*A Love For Three Oranges*. When the management of the Chicago Opera decided to produce an opera by Prokofiev, he suggested a comic opera after Gozzi. Conductor Campanini, an effusive Italian, was enthusiastic. "Gozzi! Our dearest Gozzi! Isn't that marvelous!" The composer wrote the new opera in a short time, despite a delay forced by scarlet fever and diphtheria. Suddenly, Campanini died, and the premiere was postponed. Prokofiev had to go back to exhausting recitals before unappreciative audiences, and, of all his works, the managers let him perform popular miniatures only.

Cartoon of Prokofiev in *The World Magazine*.

Life in America was beginning to distress him. "I wandered in the enormous Central Park in New York, staring at the sky-scrapers around it, thinking, in a cold fury, of the excellent American orchestras that didn't care for my music; of the critics who would repeat something that had already been repeated a hundred times, like 'Beethoven is a great composer,' and rudely ignore all novelty; of the managers arranging tours for artists who played, 50 times over, one and the same program of well-known pieces. I have come here too early; the baby (America) is too young for new music. To go home? But how? White fronts have closed around Russia on all sides; and also, it wouldn't be much of a glorious homecoming!"

In April 1920, Prokofiev went to Paris and London, where he resumed contacts with Dyaghilev and, on his advice, began to work at a remake of *The Clown*. In the fall, he toured in America again and was billed by the managers in a really annoying way: "Composer Stravinsky and pianist Prokofiev."

In the spring of 1921, Paris heard Prokofiev for the first time, with great enthusiasm. On April 29, Kussevitsky conducted *The Scythian Suite*, and on May 17, Dyaghilev's company opened the new season with the premiere of *The Tale Of The Clown Who Outwitted Seven Clowns*.

Prokofiev in a New York hotel room, in 1918.

The premiere was quite impressive. Dyaghilev had ordered a portrait of Prokofiev from Henri Matisse for the posters. The author conducted. The Parisian press appraised the music of the ballet as "a splendid introduction to Prokofiev." M. Larionov's choreography raised much argument and criticism, but even the most venerable figures of the art world joined in the enthusiastic reception of the music. Prokofiev was proud of his success: "The public here is sharp and advanced, and knows when to turn the page, not only in the score but in music in general."

The plot of the ballet develops at a fast pace in six short scenes following immediately one after the other. The hero is a slightly roguish, perky peasant. He tricks seven clowns into buying a "magical" whip from him, then, disguised as a girl, is hired by the same clowns as a cook; he gets a rich merchant to fall in love with him and fools him, too, and, after all these adventures, having made a good deal of money, returns to his Lady Clown. The humor of the tale is biting, sometimes even cruel, but, in spite of that, one is left, on the whole, with the impression of a merry show where the keen-witted hero wins over conceited fools.

The Clown is a work of distinctly national style. The ballet is Russian in character, in mischievous fun, in the dynamics of performance, and, finally, in the truly Russian quality of the music. The composer later reminisced: "...The Russian material was very easy to compose. As if I had touched upon an unexplored territory, or thrown seed into virgin land, and the new soil gave up an unexpected harvest." The grotesqueness of *The Clown*, the fairy-tale implausibility of the situations were attractive to Prokofiev. The humorous, "puppet-show" quality of the ballet determined, to a great extent, the quality of the music. The folk-style melodies are seasoned with sharp biting harmonies, astringent timbre sonorities. The seven clowns and their daughters, and the stupid Merchant are depicted in a particularly comic way.

One finds fanciful, mirthful inventiveness on every page of the score, beginning with the first, where the effect of "some whistling and rattling" is reproduced, "as if the orchestra were being dusted before the performance." In *The Clown*, Prokofiev revealed his wonderful ability to depict not only the situation but his own attitude in a few strokes—such, for instance, is the episode in the merchant's bedroom, where the comic, frivolous ambiguity of the scene is commented upon by the sneering sound of an English horn.

After having given several performances in Paris, the Dyaghilev company went to England, and, on June 9, *The Clown* premiered in London. Soon after that, Prokofiev returned to France and, in seclusion in a small town called Rochelet, in Bretagne, began to work on the "very passage-full" Concerto No. 3.

Piano Concerto No. 3 is one of the greatest achievements of this genre, not only in Prokofiev's work, but in the piano literature of the world. It is youthfulness of art, assured of its tremendous power. Emotions are spontaneous and joyous, piano techniques are brilliant and innovative. The author fervently strews striking virtuoso effects before the audience. Almost all of the thematic material of the Concerto was written in Russia. That was probably what determined the genuinely national quality of the work; that is why the themes are so simply and beautifully Russian—for instance, the clarinet theme of movement 1. The further development—grotesque, energetic, impetuous virtuosity—never obscures the broad lyrical flow of the melody. The theme for movement 2 was composed by Prokofiev as early as 1913. It combines, in a charming way, the "gavotte quality" so dear to the composer, and Russian song-like quality. The outline of the melody is austere, the movement is measured. The more unexpected is its development—in the form of variations, with their exciting contrasts, amazingly unlike each other. After the variations theme passes transparently through the coda, movement 3 brings the audience back to active and violent shapes. Central in the finale is the captivating, sweeping, passionately flowing melody, reminding one again of the breath of the Motherland.

> But then the tide arose, all-sweeping, wild and raving.
> Prokofiev! Bloom of youth and music all in one!
> You gave the orchestra the summer it was craving;
> The mighty Scythian beats his tambourine—the Sun.

So poet K. Balmont in his sonnet described Piano Concerto No. 3, admired by outstanding musicians all over the world.

In 1921, Prokofiev's "American curve" went up again. At that time, opera singer Mary Garden, unforgettable as Mélisande in Debussy's opera *Pelléas and Mélisande*, became director of the Chicago Opera. On her initiative, the theatre signed a new contract for a production of *A Love For Three Oranges*, and in October Prokofiev returned from France for the rehearsals. By winter, everything was ready for the premiere.

The premiere, on December 30, 1921, was a brilliant success.

At a rehearsal of *The Clown*.
Drawing by the renowned artist
Mikhail Larionov.

The Chicago opera theatre.

The Russian composer on a
Chicago street.

It was attended by famous American musicians and leading theatre critics. There were large headlines in the papers.

Gozzi's tale is full of lively folk humor; it challenges banality, clichés, empty "profundity" on the stage. The Italian playwright's ironic spirit appealed to Meyerhold and his sympathizers, K. Vogak and V. Solovyov, who wrote a stage version of the tale. They introduced an allegorical Prologue where amusing characters were arguing: the Tragics, the Comics, the Empty-heads and the Eccentrics. Each group stands for a specific theatrical genre. Throughout the performance, these "representatives of the audience" demand, in accordance with their preferences, "Healthy laughter! Cheerful atmosphere!" or "Sorrow! Tears! Murders! Suffering fathers! Revelations of the meaning!" The leading characters are comic: the King, very majestic, but not without a sense of humor; Truffaldino, the "jesting person"; pompous Magician Celio, in whose miraculous powers no one believes, not even himself; the Cook, gigantic and terrifying, with her enormous soup ladle and her hoarse bass; the young Prince, at first unbearably boring, sickly, "hypochondriac," and then, after the sudden cure by laughter, passionately in love, full of determination and courage. As the plot develops at breathtaking speed, incredible situations and amusing adventures follow one another, and merry laughter— "the leading character of the opera," according to Asafiev—hovers over everything.

Prokofiev's music in the opera is joyful and life-affirming. The characters' recitative cues, the ironic echoes in the orchestra, the harsh and biting timbre combinations are full of comic spirit.

"To each, his own pace and intonation," Asafiev wrote, commenting on the characters' distinctive individuality. The leitmotifs, the short phrases or the heroes' longer utterances outline not only their personalities but their manner of speaking, moving, gesticulating.

Throughout the opera, a serious, impassioned and intense fight between two worlds is going on. The evil and powerful Fata Morgana, with the help of her accomplice Smeraldine, patronizes the evil-doing Leandre and Clarice, who want the Prince dead. On the Prince's side are his loyal friend, merry Truffaldino, as well as the King and the courtiers. The fantastic characters are represented by easily recognizable means: the leitmotif with the characteristic opening triplet, sharp thick chords, loud and booming timbres. The real-life characters are depicted by clear and melodious music—in consideration of the tastes of American audiences, Prokofiev "chose a musical language simpler than that of *The Gambler*." One certainly appealing thing about the heroes is that they are always ready to break into a dance. Truffaldino dances as he tries to make the hypochondriac ailing Prince laugh; the Little Devils hop in a "hellish" dance; the courtiers dance with happiness when, incredibly, the Prince is cured. The magnificent festive March, which immediately became world-known, established itself as the musical emblem of the opera.

After a successful premiere of *A Love For Three Oranges*, a sud-

A 16th-century engraving from the program of *The Angel Of Fire*.

den failure followed when the opera was performed in New York. "They were like a pack of dogs who jumped at me suddenly from a gateway and tore at my pants," Prokofiev wrote about the New York reviewers. Along with a disappointment in the American public, there was "a wish to go and work somewhere in a quiet place."

In March 1922, Prokofiev went to Germany with his mother and settled in Ettal, a village in the picturesque Bavarian Alps. There, he hoped to have a good rest after the last three years' wanderings, and "to do some good work: have *Three Oranges* printed, and complete another opera" – *The Angel Of Fire*, after the novel by Valery Bryusov.

Life flowed, slow and orderly, in the provincial Bavarian village and was beneficial to his work. In the nearby village of Oberammergau, old mystery plays, "The Passions of Christ" were performed once in ten years. Prokofiev was able to attend such a performance. "I sat down to work on *The Angel Of Fire*; by the way, the witches' covens described in it were held somewhere in this neighborhood." It was not until 1927, however, that the opera was completed. Sadly enough, the composer never lived to see *The Angel Of Fire* produced on stage.

The action in *The Angel of Fire*, libretto published in 1908, takes place in medieval Germany, in the dark age of the Inquisition when, all over Europe, women accused of sorcery were burned. The heroine is the passionate, troubled Renata, smitten with love for the Angel of Fire, Madiel. Renata is convinced that Madiel has been incarnated in Count Heinrich, who has spurned her love. Renata raves insanely, haunted by visions of the Angel of Fire. Knight Ruprecht, who is in love with Renata, tries to help her cast the insane passion away. But his efforts are useless. Renata goes to a nunnery, but the Angel of Fire continues to haunt her. The Inquisition accuses Renata of witchcraft and condemns her to be burned at the stake.

Prokofiev the artist was always drawn to violent passions and strong, uncommon characters. What he valued most in Bryusov's story was not the colorful description of mystical visions or witch-burnings, but the tragedy of Renata, and Ruprecht's self-sacrificing struggle to cure her mind. At the center of the tale is the heroine with her troubled spirit, her all-consuming love. "After the light and mirthful *Oranges*, it was quite challenging to switch to the passionate, searching Renata." Renata's vocal part is rich in lengthy, tonally intense structures and powerful culminations. One is deeply impressed by Renata's incantations, by the extensive story she tells in the beginning of the opera – now calm narration, now violent emotional outbursts – and also, by the imperious manner in which Renata addresses the Inquisitor in the last scene.

Most unforgettable are the episodes where Prokofiev, freely using a rich palette of orchestral and vocal resources, depicts the illusory, and therefore all the more terrible, world of gloomy black-magic fantasy. Such is the last scene of the opera. Renata's mystical ecstasy spreads to the other nuns. Some invoke the vi-

A scene from *A Love for Three Oranges* (1964 production at the MALEGOT in Leningrad).

Truffaldino and the Cook (from *A Love for Three Oranges*). "In my *Oranges* they found mockery, challenge, grotesque, and all I had in mind was a merry show."

From the production of *The Angel Of Fire* at the International Festival of Modern Music in Venice in 1955.

sion of Madiel, some pronounce incantations, trying to cast off the haunting nightmare, some curse Renata. The gradual accumulation of the entering female voices creates a sonorous torrent of tremendous power. Renata's voice and the ascetic intonations of the Inquisitor's incantations join in the storming avalanche of sound. The scene concludes with the terrible sentence on the heroine.

The fervent humanistic pathos of *The Angel Of Fire* and Prokofiev's perfect artistic mastery never failed to delight those who heard this work, the composer's favorite. "You know what stuns me?" Myaskovsky wrote. "The astonishing, if one may say so, humaneness of your music and the images it creates. The figures of Ruprecht and Renata—that is not theatre, and even less opera; they are real, living people, so profound and genuine are all their intonations . . . To present characters like Ruprecht and Renata in their total depth and amazingly human complexity, one must be a full, mature genius."

The period of work on *The Angel Of Fire* was a happy time in Prokofiev's life. He was resting from his busy life in America, packed with endless concert tours. The quiet and the lovely nature of Southern Germany were favorable to creative work. There, in Ettal, Prokofiev married young Spanish singer Lina Codina (her stage name was Lina Llubera). For eighteen years, Lina shared the composer's hectic life; she became the mother of his two sons. A gifted singer, she often performed Prokofiev's vocal works.

The Ettal idyll ended in the fall of 1923, when Prokofiev and his now larger family moved to Paris.

*   *   *

In the 1920s, Paris had no equal in brilliant and numerous talents. People went there to find success and fame, to breathe the fragrance of the gorgeous city and express a fraction of its uniqueness in their art. There were many of them—those who were lured by the glittering lights of Paris in a dedicated endeavor to create new art. There was a premiere every day, a debut every evening, introducing a new name. Artists loved Paris more than America: Parisians were no less sophisticated, but they were also more enthusiastic; they were always ready to make new idols.

Here, they followed the development of Stravinsky's enchanting talent, revered the venerable Ravel, gaped at Picasso's innovations, admired the music of young French composers. The glories of Paris were, in those years, Cocteau and Honegger, Shalyapin and Dyaghilev, Casella and Milhaud, Matisse and Goncharova. Chaplin spent much of his time here (he will call one of his best films, *The Woman Of Paris*). Every day, early in the morning, the young reporter Ernest Hemingway went to a small cafe to write his first stories. He will write a book of reminiscences about Paris and call it *The Moveable Feast*.

The musicians, artists, writers of that time were determined to refute the esthetics of the art of the recent past, to break down its established foundations. In his brilliantly written manifesto,

The village of Ettal. Prokofiev drew an arrow pointing at "our country house."

"The Cock And The Harlequin: Notes On Music," Jean Cocteau attacked the artistic credo of Impressionism and outlined the aspirations of the new generation of composers. "Enough of clouds, waves, aquariums, naiads, nightly fragrances. We want earthly music, music of day-to-day life. We want sharp and resolute music ... To be truthful, one must be firm ..." The compositions one heard in Paris in the 20s stunned by their thematic variety and diversity. The Biblical subject matter in Honegger's operas and oratorios bear the mark of intense spiritual searching. Milhaud's "minute-opera" parodies, young Poulenc's gracious, delightful, life-celebrating ballets, written about the same time, are obviously entertaining. The music of stadiums, sports-rings, modern city streets can be heard beside Stravinsky's works that resurrect the imagery and style of Baroque art. The 1920s were a period of relative stability and prosperity in the life of European society. A keen sensitivity to the pleasures of life, a craving for happiness and fun gave birth to the numerous flashy premieres of entertainment dancing shows, acrobatic pantomimes, music-hall revues.

Young Prokofiev basked in the Parisian sun. "... French musical circles instantly recognized this blond man with such an open face and such a generous smile," René Dumesnil recollected in the mid-40s. Exciting acquaintances, unforgettable encounters, stunning impressions ... He became friendly with young French composers, with chessmasters Capablanca and Alyokhin, with artists Petrov-Vodkin and Benoît. Each performance of his works became a notable event in cultural life, his compositions were widely published. Prokofiev's tours abroad covered almost the entire world. Some of the most famous personalities of the art world were among his friends.

Prokofiev's forceful individuality, however, was not overpowered by the abundance of striking impressions. Implicit in the composer's statements is a critical attitude to much of what he saw and heard, a firm determination to preserve his own original style. Endeavoring to assert his independence, Prokofiev expressed provocative, sometimes harsh opinions on music by contemporary composers. "Too cerebral," "Bechmesserianism" – on Hindemith; "a kind of indifference, lack of life" – on Weill's Violin Concerto; "boring nonsense" – on works by American composers. His former pride in having been the first to perform Schoenberg's piano compositions in Russia (Prokofiev played two pieces from op. 11 in the 1910/11 season of the "Soirees of Modern Music") gave way to an indifferent attitude to the achievements of the New Viennese.

Prokofiev flatly rejected the emptiness and meaninglessness into which French composers sometimes lapse in their works. "In certain Parisian circles, they have been saying lately: we've had enough of tragic and emotional music, we want entertaining music, just like in good old Rameau's time, and if, for the sake of entertainment, there is a bit of tastelessness, let's have that, too, if it's appropriate and entertaining!" But such moods were alien to the Russian composer. He "went against the stream" in Paris just

Portrait of Prokofiev by Ostroumova-Lebedeva.

Prokofiev and his wife, singer Lina
Llubera.

Drawing of Prokofiev by the great
French artist Henri Matisse.

as consistently as he had held up his originality in Russia, and would do so throughout his entire life.

The noisy urban atmosphere did nothing to change the composer's strict working regime. Habits acquired as a child helped him to work tirelessly under any conditions, overcoming all obstacles. The life of Prokofiev's family was totally subordinated to Sergei Sergeievich's work. The fame of a composer in vogue did not produce a very high income, and so they often had to economize, moving from one residence to another—a permanent apartment in Paris was too expensive. In February 1924, the Prokofievs had a son, Svyatoslav. Several months later, a tragedy befell the composer: Mariya Grigorievna died. In the last years of her life, ill and blind, she continued to devote herself to her son's affairs and interests. Her deteriorating health did not allow her to help him as she always had; she only had time to write memoirs about the composer's childhood. Throughout his life, Prokofiev had deep affection for his mother, and immense gratitude for all the efforts she had made to encourage and develop his talent. The loss of the one who, of all people, had been the closest to him, was extremely painful to the composer.

Summer, as usual, was spent in tireless work, with short periods of rest. The Prokofievs visited quiet country places, where the composer realized his most important projects. Contacts with friends—music-making with Poulenc and Février, conversations about art with artists Petrov-Vodkin and Benoît —helped him in his work. In 1926, the artist Ostroumova-Lebedeva came from Leningrad for a visit to Paris; she did an interesting portrait of Prokofiev.

The diversity and richness of stylistic devices in the works Prokofiev composed in Paris is quite impressive. His determination to be himself, not to give in to the pressure of "Parisian spells" is undoubtedly combined with assimilation of the most significant achievements of modern compositional technique. One cannot imagine a truly great artist who does not unify and fuse, in his own individuality, the artistic impressions of his time. In his best compositions of the Paris period, Prokofiev successfully grasped and expressed in his own unique language the best, the most original and the most characteristic qualities of Western European music of the 1920s.

The decade Prokofiev spent in Paris opened with the premiere of the Violin Concerto. Composed several years earlier, it was performed on the day the composer arrived in the capital of France. Here, after the voluntary seclusion in Ettal, were the crowded boxes of the Grand Opera, a splendid audience that included K. Szymanowski, A. Rubinstein, J. Szigeti, P. Picasso, A. Benoît, A. Pavlova. The wonderful music of the Concerto, with its romantically striking contrasts, its sublime lyricism, was not received well by the Parisians. The Concerto was criticized for old-fashioned romanticism, even for "Mendelssohnism." Thus, from the very beginning, Paris was dictating to the composer its own rules which had to be reckoned with. And so, the next premiere introduced the Prokofiev who astounded the audience

Prokofiev in his garden.

with the primeval power of the Cantata *They Are Seven*, with the stunning contrasts of the chromatic Sonata No. 5 (which, nevertheless, was not a success because of its serenely wise narrative style). It took Prokofiev much time and energy to make the new version of Piano Concerto No. 2 ready for the premiere, but the composition was received "with reserve." The romantic coloring of the music, its open expressiveness were regarded in Paris as obsolete and not representative of Prokofiev.

In June 1923, Myaskovsky wrote in a letter, speaking of his new Symphony No. 7, that it is "very impetuous, and disgustingly false, and will obviously fail to please your *'diatonic'* (italics by N.S.) taste . . ." For Myaskovsky, the "diatonicism" of Prokofiev's thinking consisted of those qualities of his talent determined by the clarity of language, the life-affirming, dynamic tone of his music. "I must admit I sometimes use your music for a hygienic purpose: after you have swallowed a bellyfull of all those Bartóks, Welleszes, Kreneks, Poulencs, Groszes, Hindemiths, etc. . . . — there is an urgent need to go out and breathe the fresh and healthy air of your domain." The uniqueness of Prokofiev's gift, a gift unlike anything that was valued abroad at that time, made it somewhat difficult to establish a rapport with audiences and the press. The music one heard in Paris called for a complicated, drily logical art, distant from simplicity of feeling and expression. Such art was alien to Prokofiev. Yet there were things in new post-war music that had much in common with his own aspirations.

"I have decided to write a large symphony, 'made of steel and iron . . .' " He conceived a symphony in two movements, "the first an angry allegro, allegro ben articolato, the second a theme with variations." This conscious decision to write a complicated "thing of steel" impeded the process of composition. In March 1925, Prokofiev wrote to Myaskovsky: "After some desperate messing about, I have completed the orchestration of the first movement of the symphony. It took about a hundred pages, covered with writing from top to bottom."

Symphony No. 2, some episodes of which were begun in the summer of 1924, was completed on May 22, 1925 and, two weeks later, performed at a Kussevitsky concert. Neither the premiere, nor the few subsequent performances had any success at the time. ". . . It was too thickly woven together; there were too many phrase overlaps, too many counterpoints changing into figurations." The symphony's failure distressed the composer, but he did not want to believe all that effort had been wasted. "There still is a hope, deep down, that in a few years the symphony will prove to be a decent and even harmonious thing. Is it possible that, at my age, I have stumbled, from the height of all my technique, into such a mess — and after 9 months of relentless work, too?"

Critics were united against the symphony; the Parisians, usually so enthusiastic about each new extravagant opus, found nothing in this composition but frighteningly thunderous chords, thickly interwoven complex structures, barbaric urbanisms. It was only

Poster for a performance of Prokofiev's Symphony no. 2.

Prokofiev with his mother Mariya
Grigorievna (shortly before her
death), wife Lina, and little son.

Drawing of Prokofiev made by the
famous artist Natalia Goncharova
in Paris.

decades after the premiere of this work that what the first audiences had probably failed to discern became evident.

In the first movement, through harsh sonorous structures "of steel and iron," images of Russian folk-tales, Russian antiquity appear. The sweeping power, the austere simplicity of old hymns, the rebellious Scythian spirit are combined, in a striking way, with hypertrophied sonorities inspired by the dynamic motion of modern techniques.

The low, soft orchestra figurations open the second movement—the theme with variations. "After the dynamic first movement, I wanted some relaxation at least in the beginning of the second, which I had conceived as a theme with variations, and for that I used a tranquil theme I had composed in Japan." The opening oboe melody is enchanting; its light, melodic quality is especially compelling after the deafening sonorities of movement 1. The six variations that follow alter the theme beyond recognition. In them, Prokofiev breaks free of the fetters of conscious complicatedness; this is the Prokofiev of the future *Romeo and Juliet* pages. Gracious pastoral tableaux, merry though not too refined dances follow one after another. The chaste, delicate, moving lyricism of the central (fourth) variation serves as a foil for the subsequent powerful accumulation of tension. The general culmination of the composition is an avalanche of stern sonorities, with the dynamics of movement 1 underlying it. And yet, the triumph of the soulless forces of steel is not the conclusion of the symphony. In the serene, tranquil postscript to the grandiose structure, the variations-theme comes back, a soft and pure ending to the extraordinary cycle.

In the summer of 1925, Prokofiev received a surprising offer. Sergei Dyaghilev wanted a ballet about Soviet Russia. "I couldn't believe my own ears. It was like a window opening into the fresh air Lunacharsky had spoke of." Working on the ballet was, to the composer, a joyous participation in the new life, and he set about his work enthusiastically. Prokofiev wanted to have Ilya Ehrenburg, who was then in France, write the libretto. But it could not be arranged, and artist G. Yakulov, whose works were quite a success in Paris, was brought in as scriptwriter. He explained the contents of the ballet for which Dyaghilev found a striking, uncommon title, *The Step of Steel.* "There are two acts in the ballet: the breakdown and disintegration of the old lifestyle, with the revolutionaries' enthusiasm shown against the background of this dissolution; and the pathos of labor, organized from inside and from outside."

The premiere, carefully prepared by Dyaghilev, was held in Paris on May 7, 1927 in the Sarah Bernhardt theatre. It was attended by Ravel, Stravinsky, Picasso. At the performance in London, members of the royal family were present. Prokofiev commented with particular satisfaction on the production of the ballet in the Metropolitan Theatre in New York: "It was quite interesting to see a huge red banner soar on the stage of this most bourgeois of all bourgeois theatres."

The authors of 'The Step Of Steel' were trying to convey their

Model of stage set for *The Step of Steel,* by G.B. Yakulov.

own idea of the new modern Russia. Unusual characters appeared on the stages of European and American theatres: the Public Speaker, the Woman Worker, the Sailor who then becomes a Worker, Sweets Salesmen, Cigarette Salesmen. The "heroes" of the recent past—speculators and hoarders—gave place, in the second act, to the builders of the future. The authors' imagination pictured the new Russia as a powerful industrial country. The dream of the future was scenically realized as an apotheosis of technology. In the last part of the ballet, there were humming machines, rotating shafts, never-stopping mechanisms on the stage. Dancers acted as rhythmically toiling people, and sometimes their movements were indistinguishable from those of the machines. It had been conceived that way, "to create the impression of useful 'toil,' not abstract choreography," Yakulov wrote, commenting on the stage set design.

Prokofiev composed the music as if trying to confirm the statement he had made in a letter to Myaskovsky, shortly after the premiere of Symphony No. 2: "Anyway—Schluss ('finished'—German)—now, they won't get anything complicated from me for a long time." Without quoting, the composer turned to rhythms and intonations of popular verses, simple city songs, merry dances. The ringing timbres of the orchestra, the simple "white-key" melodies, with occasional sharper intonations, the multilayered overlappings of evenly moving voices—such is the music of 'The Step of Steel.'

The cheerful, life-affirming music gave a picture of the coming world as it was envisioned by the composer who hadn't seen his country for a long time but whose thoughts were always with it. (The ballet, Asafiev wrote, expressed "the true style of our era, for here, one may speak of hammered rhythms, of steel-like resilient intonations, of musical ebb and flow, like gigantic bellows breathing!"). After the premiere, Prokofiev was branded as "an apostle of Bolshevism." White emigre papers were in a rage: "A prickly flower of Proletcult (Soviet abbreviation for Proletarian Culture) ministers!" European critics permanently affixed the "Red composer" label on Prokofiev.

The winter of 1925 is notable for the Prokofievs' trip to the U.S., a tour through the major cities. Sergei Sergeievich performed his own works, and also served as accompanist to Lina Llubera who sang songs by Russian composers.

The tour of fourteen concerts was a success. Prokofiev conquered America the way many other artists had—having first achieved a strong reputation in Europe.

After youthful, exuberant America, it was nice to see once more the sweet nature and the beautiful art of Italy. "Besides the sun, the Rafaels, Vesuvius and the blooming orange trees, I saw Gorky and Vyacheslav Ivanov," the composer reminisced later. At a matinee recital in Naples, a surprise was awaiting the composer: Gorky came to the artists' room. Alexey Maksimovich took the Prokofievs to his home for dinner. According to Lina Llubera, his long stories about life in the Soviet Union were so captivating that "one could listen for hours."

Sergei Prokofiev and Lina Llubera-Prokofieva in 1927.

During breaks between never-ending tours, in the short hours of rest after intense creative work, Prokofiev acted as cordial host to such guests as C. Chaplin, F. Shalyapin, L. Stokowsky, chessmasters R. Capablanca, A. Alyokhin. In summer, he spent much time on a new hobby—the motor-car. The composer went on exciting trips through France and Switzerland, admiring the beauty of nature and old architecture: ". . . France is lovely and soft, and in the mountains, one finds deep underground caves . . ." Sometimes, V. Sofronitzky, V. Meyerhold, novelist and playwright A. Afinogenov, on their visits to France, would take turns in joining Prokofiev on these trips. Since the mid-20s, life in Paris was continually brightened by visits from friends and acquaintances coming from Soviet Russia. Among them were old friends and fellow-students B. Zakharov and B. Asafiev. Unfortunately, Nikolai Yakovlevich Myaskovsky, whom Sergei Sergeievich was so eager to see, was too busy to come. Prokofiev kept in touch with Soviet artists K. Petrov-Vodkin and G. Yakulov, met I. Ehrenburg. Some people remember that Prokofiev and Mayakovsky, who often met in Paris, were very close to each other: "When Mayakovsky listened to Sergei Sergeievich playing the piano, he would relax, and, all of a sudden, his eyes would light up warmly."

In those years, Prokofiev's music became increasingly popular in the Soviet Union. The merry opera *A Love For Three Oranges* was produced in Leningrad and Moscow, the majestic Concerto No. 3 was performed by S. Feinberg and L. Oborin; in concert halls, the *Scythian Suite* was performed by the "Firsymphense"—the First Symphony Ensemble without a conductor. The growing interest in his music led to the first negotiations on practical issues—about a production of *The Gambler*, about joining the Moscow Composers' Society, about a possible tour.

In July 1925, the Presidium of the Central Executive Committee of the U.S.S.R. Commission on the commemoration of the 1905 Revolution twentieth anniversary held a conference, attended by Meyerhold and Eisenstein. Among other things, it was resolved: "The pageant planned by the commission will include a production of the film *1905*, based on the script now in preparation by N. Shutko . . . Com. Meyerhold will be requested, during his assignment trip abroad, to contact composer S. Prokofiev and negotiate about Prokofiev's return to the U.S.S.R. and about work on the cinesymphony, and inform this commission of the conditions." The idea of getting Prokofiev to cooperate was, unfortunately, never carried out; and the project of a film for the twentieth anniversary of the 1905 Revolution was later made into *Battleship Potemkin*, directed by Sergei Eisenstein.

In January 1927, a happy, long-expected event took place in Prokofiev's life: he made a trip to Soviet Russia. For the first time, after a ten-year absence, he was able to see all the great changes his friends had told him about in their letters, to see how much the Soviet people loved and valued his music.

On the very day he arrived in Moscow, the composer held an orchestra rehearsal with the "Firsymphense." When Sergei

Prokofiev with a group of Soviet musicians.

Sergeievich walked into the hall, the March from *A Love For Three Oranges* burst forth—the animated musicians were greeting the composer. Prokofiev, as usual, was serious, businesslike, stern. The audience that gathered in the Grand Hall of the Moscow Conservatory for the first recital received him enthusiastically. Even more successful were the performances in Leningrad. At the GATOB (formerly the Mariinsky Theatre) production of *A Love For Three Oranges*, Prokofiev heard the opera together with Lunacharsky, who admiringly compared it to a glass of champagne. "This is the first real production of the opera; it has talent and life; it is much superior to the New York, Chicago, Berlin and Cologne productions," the composer remarked, pleased both by the careful interpretation of the music and by the beautiful, fanciful stage production.

There were several appearances in the Ukraine. The visit from a world-famous musician made an unforgettable impression on the Kharkov, Kiev and Odessa audiences. There were some amusing incidents, too. Young David Oistrakh was performing the scherzo from the Violin Concerto, and the composer gave him a good dressing-down. Oistrakh recollected: "He strode towards the stage, asked the pianist to give him his seat, and saying to me, 'This is absolutely not the right way to play it, young man,' began to demonstrate and explain to me the nature of his music. It was a scandal . . ." One of Prokofiev's recitals in Odessa was heard by Svyatoslav Richter—at that time, a twelve-year-old schoolboy, future unrivalled performer of Prokofiev's piano works.

The trip, almost two months long, was packed with recitals, theatre attendances, meetings with musicians. He was particularly impressed by twenty-year-old Dmitry Shostakovich. On his return to Paris, Sergei Sergeievich continued to popularize works by Soviet composers in the West, and added to them the works of the talented young generation.

The Prokofievs stayed for two days at Asafiev's house in the Detskoye Selo near Leningrad; Nikolai Yakovlevich Myaskovsky came there, too. Meeting again, not far from the city where they had spent their youth, the friends discussed music for hours, remembered the Conservatory, the Petrograd of the memorable pre-revolutionary years. It was a short break in the exhausting, busy tour. Prokofiev went back to Paris feeling younger and more alive. Lina Prokofieva remembers: "We were seen off by friends, old and new, it was quite moving; and we were saying, 'good-bye, see you soon,' full of so many exciting impressions to take back with us."

The Staatsoper of Berlin took an interest in *The Angel Of Fire* and planned to produce the opera in the 1926/27 season, but the production was not completed. Annoyed, the composer decided to give the music of *The Angel Of Fire* a fresh start as a symphony. "Just imagine," he wrote to Myaskovsky in August 1928, "the material I have selected from it fit, quite unexpectedly, into a four-part symphony form!" Of all the works written by him abroad, it is difficult to find another with as striking a depth, power and passion of feeling. Prokofiev included the best

A scene from *The Angel Of Fire*, produced in Köln (West Germany), in 1960.

A scene from *The Step of Steel*.

Prokofiev in the Detskoye Selo
with Asafiev, in 1927.

fragments of the opera—Renata's story, the music of the duel between Ruprecht and Count Heinrich—in the new Symphony No. 3. The listener familiar with the music of the opera discovers with some surprise that some of the themes sound slightly different in the Symphony—one can clearly hear intonations of slow, drawn-out Russian folk songs. Warm, pathetic episodes contrast with those parts where a formidable, disturbing force storms out. This combination gives the symphony its unique spirit, full of drama, anxiety, profound humaneness.

The spring of 1929 is noteworthy for the appearance of another choreographic work. The ballet *The Prodigal Son* is the last joint project of Prokofiev and Dyaghilev.

Towards the end of the famous impresario's life, the evolution of his aspirations took yet another turn. Now, it was not magnificent, extravagant, sensation-seasoned pageants that he deemed important, but those works of art that speak of simple, and therefore unchanging and great values of human life—honesty, sincerity, love for hearth and home.

The ancient story of the prodigal son, the simple and genuine human drama is revealed without affectation, with reserve and expressiveness. Here, the aspirations of Dyaghilev, approaching his sixtieth birthday, fully coincided with those of Prokofiev, who was in search of natural emotional expression and simplicity. ("I aspire for greater simplicity and melodiousness," he would say in an interview two years later.) The composer wrote marvelous, sincere, humane music for the ballet, music full of unsubdued, poetic beauty. The score seems to depict two different forces of life. The world of a sincere young soul, its aspirations, dreams, hopes and sufferings are shown with especially warm, delicate tones. Melodies are songlike and gracious, the web of music transparent and, at some moments, ethereal. Such are the lyrical duets, which characterize the Beauty. The force of violent emotions, an active, warlike principle, is represented through energetic rhythms (the "Robbery" or "Sharing the booty" episodes). Prokofiev was fond of the music of *The Prodigal Son* and turned to it many times. A year after the premiere, he wrote Symphony No. 4, based on the ballet's thematic construction—a vast epic picture, rich in contrasting images and discordant themes, but whole and unified in style.

The premiere of *The Prodigal Son* was a success, but two months later, Dyaghilev died suddenly in Venice. The complex, not always smooth nature of the relationship between him and Prokofiev did not prevent the composer from deeply revering the work of this enthusiastic champion of Russian art. Prokofiev saw Dyaghilev's death as "the loss of a colossal and certainly unique figure that becomes even larger in size as it is farther away from us."

In November 1929, the composer went once more to the U.S.S.R. He spent three weeks in Moscow and saw the new Bolshoi Theatre production of *A Love For Three Oranges*; there was talk about a production of *The Step Of Steel*; unfortunately, these plans were not realized. Just before the New Year, Prokofiev and his wife went on yet another tour through U.S. cities.

Prokofiev performing in Moscow in 1927 (drawing by G.S. Vereysky).

The twenty-five recitals throughout the country were a tremendous success. "It seems that, by and by, they have been converted to believe in me," the composer noted with satisfaction.

The trip was full of exotic impressions: the crossing of the Mississippi river; the Arizona desert; Niagara Falls. He spent several days in Cuba. There, Spanish poet and revolutionary Federico García Lorca attended a Prokofiev recital. Delighted by the composer's piano pieces, Lorca had a long conversation with him in the Vedado hotel, where the Prokofievs were staying. Prokofiev was enchanted by the luxurious exotic vegetation and the wonderful warm tropical sea. And yet, he wrote: "Palm trees, Southern seas—all that is exquisitely beautiful; and yet, I have a Northern soul, and I wouldn't like to live here."

One cannot fail to mention an encounter that happened earlier, on his way to America. On board the transatlantic ocean liner "Berengaria," fate brought Prokofiev and Rachmaninov together —two Russians far away from their homeland. The one who was twenty years younger was to return to Russia, to devote his work and talent to her. The other—the one who had been called "the idol of Moscow" in his youth—never again crossed Russian borders. Images of his native country haunted Rachmaninov painfully throughout his life. During the war, on the threshold of death, he contributed the box-office profits from his recitals to the benefit of the Red Army, and wrote: "Possible assistance from a Russian to the Russian people in its struggle against the enemy." And now, Rachmaninov asked countless questions, and a hidden nostalgia can be felt in those questions . . .

Prokofiev felt more and more acutely the necessity of new contacts with Soviet Russia. He kept track of all the news eagerly, read books by Soviet writers. He corresponded extensively with old friends, helped them; at Asafiev's request, for instance, he found folk-lore material of the French Revolution era, for the forthcoming ballet *The Flames Of Paris*.

Most of the works Prokofiev wrote in the latter years of his life abroad are not connected with musical theatre (except for the one-act ballet *On The Dnieper*). By that time, the composer had not only achieved the heights of artistic mastery, but acquired experience and wisdom in life. He was ready to give life to subjects of high civic ideals, to stories of great events and strong characters. But his milieu offered no such subjects or stories. And so, the late 20s and the early 30s are a period when he created instrumental compositions: Symphony No. 4 (based on the ballet *The Prodigal Son*), Piano Concertos No. 4 (left-hand) and No. 5, String Quartet, written on commission from the Library of Congress in Washington, D.C. These works exhibit certain tendencies that Prokofiev himself defined as a search for "new simplicity." In his opinion, it was only after mastering all the complexities of compositional technique that one can achieve the ability to "express oneself in a new, yet simple way."

But the struggle to achieve the precision of style characteristic of his works of the Soviet period, was hard. In those years, the artist, indefatigable in his seeking, was left without strong

At a rehearsal of *The Prodigal Son* (drawing by Mikhail Larionov).

". . .As conductor, Prokofiev also made a remarkable impression. Prokofiev is a pianist; he felt much less at ease at the conducting stand than at the piano. And yet his conducting (of his own works) reminded one of a speaker who does not posess 'the art of eloquence' but is convincing through the sheer power of logic and by what he has to say."

Heinrich Neuhaus

Scenes from *The Prodigal Son*.

Prokofiev with the producers and
the cast of *A Love for Three
Oranges* (the GATOB, Leningrad,
1926). "The performance. . . was
brilliant, both in its symmetry and
in the realization of the composer's
desires," wrote Prokofiev.

creative stimuli. In the articles and reviews of altogether favorable French critics, there was more and more mention of dry rationality, scholasticism. Sincere, well-wishing even in his sharpest criticisms, Nikolai Yakovlevich Myaskovsky was among those who perceived signs of danger. "It seems that an element of *caution* has appeared in your work—it is especially obvious in the endings of your latest works, in the Sonatinas, for instance, where I can feel some kind of artificiality."

Prokofiev himself was well aware of the causes of his growing depression; he also knew the cure. "I must merge, once more, with the atmosphere of my native land. I must see, once more, real winters, and spring that breaks out at once. I must hear Russian speech, I must talk to people of my own flesh and blood, those who can give me back what I lack here: their songs, my songs. Here, I am losing strength. I am in danger of perishing of academicism. Yes, my friend, I am going back. . . ." Sergei Sergeievich said to his Parisian friend Serge Moreux.

The decision was made.

Prokofiev. A drawing by P. Pasquier. (Paris, 1930).

Back In The Homeland

The 1930s are an unforgettable era in Soviet history. The first socialist country in the world was going through a time of radical changes that left their mark everywhere—in social, economic and cultural life. New plants, factories, electric power stations rose as majestic monuments to the labor and enthusiasm of the Soviet people. Creative arts flourished. Novels by M. Sholokhov, L. Leonov, V. Katayev, I. Ehrenburg, F. Panferov, N. Ostrovsky, plays by V. Vishnevsky, N. Pogodin, A. Korneichuk tell of people whose character has been formed by the new conditions of life.

The scope of the creative work of cinematographers was wide and diverse: some films were based on the historic revolutionary past of Russia (*Chapaev, Lenin In October, Lenin In 1918*), some, on immortal literary classics (*The Thunderstorm, Girl Without A Dowry* by A. Ostrovsky, *Iudushka Golovlev* after M. Saltikov-Shedrin), some glorified the heroism of the Soviet people (*The Encounter, Komsomolsk*).

Drama and musical theatre, too, were going through a period of enthusiastic renewal. The symphonies of Myaskovsky and Shostakovich, talented works in cantata-oratorical genre won world fame and recognition for Russian music. And Prokofiev, intensely searching in those years for new, up-to-date, large-scale subjects, could not fail to experience the tremendous healthy influence of the achievements of Soviet art.

Prokofiev spent some time shuttling back and forth between Moscow and Paris. By the summer of 1936, the family finally moved to Moscow, with all their belongings. They had not quite settled down yet—the family had to stay in a hotel awaiting an apartment—but everybody quickly became adjusted—above all Sergei Sergeievich himself, who held consultations for Conservatory students there, in the "Natsional" hotel.

From the very first months of life in his native country, Prokofiev was extraordinarily active. He was enthusiastic to know and understand the new Russia closer and better. On his many tours through the cities of the Ukraine, Armenia, the Urals, the composer never ceased to admire the culture and responsiveness of Soviet audiences. Thus, after one of his tours, he wrote in the newspaper *Vechernyaya Moskva (Evening Moscow)*: "I must say that the workers of Chelyabinsk have shown much more interest

Moscow (the Theater Square) in the 1930s.

Dyaghilev.

Rachmaninov in the 1920s.

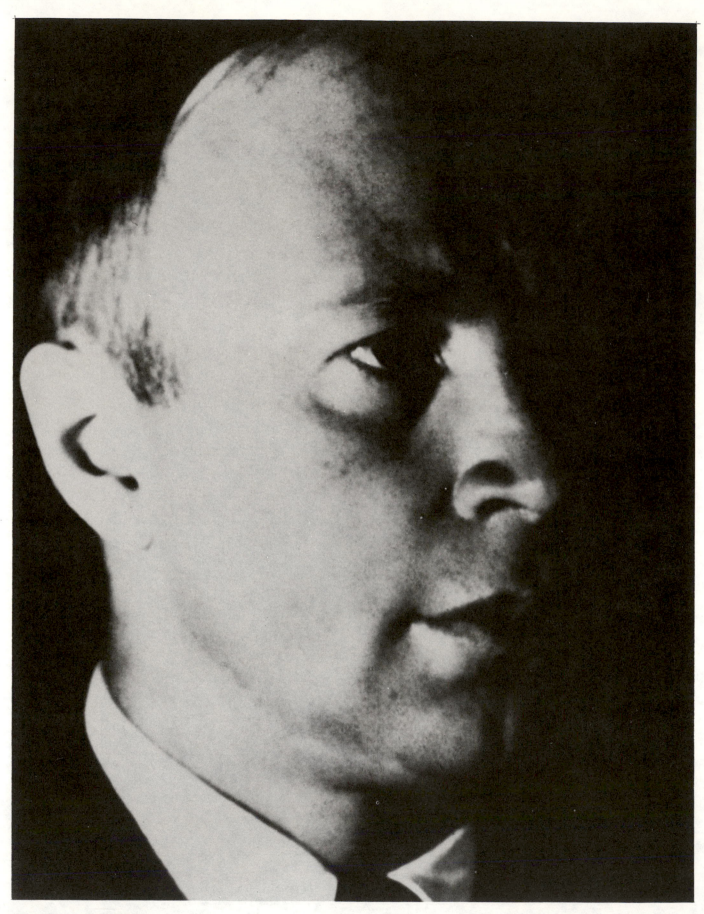

Prokofiev in the 1930s.

Prokofiev and the celebrated
violinist David Oistrakh.

in the program than some qualified audiences of West European and American centers."

Prokofiev tried to take advantage of any pause in his work to see more of the country he loved. Automobile trips along the Voyenno-Gruzinskaya road, along the Kama and Belaya rivers, through the Urals, left unforgettable impressions. Much of his time was devoted to his work as a member of the administration of the Moscow Union of Composers, to frequent attendance at theatre and concert premieres, and also to his hobbies, of which the principal one was chess. In November 1937, he played against David Oistrakh – also an excellent chess player – at an artists' club. Oistrakh remembers: "The game was played by all the rules – with regimented time, with a committee of judges and, of course, in public. Each set was followed by sleepless nights, both of us so agitated as if world championship were at stake."

Immediately after his arrival, Prokofiev began to work for cinema and theatre productions. His first experiment in the field was music for the film *Lieutenant Kizhe*, produced at the Leningrad "Belgoskino" studio after Yuri Tinyanov's novella. The composer was thrilled by the amusing plot, the satirical characters and situations. The music he wrote for the film was witty, full of subtle parody.

Prokofiev's theatrical works include *The Egyptian Nights*, produced by A. Ya. Tairov in the Kamerny (Chamber) Theatre, based on fragments from Pushkin's poem "The Egyptian Nights," Shakespeare's tragedy *Anthony and Cleopatra*, Bernard Shaw's play *Caesar and Cleopatra*. The spirit of anxiety and uneasiness that pervaded the performance derived mostly from Prokofiev's music; the music was crucial. The rich, diverse images of Tairov's production – Egypt falling prey to the crude Roman conquerors, beautiful Cleopatra, courageous Anthony – is depicted in striking, lush colors. *The Egyptian Nights* was immortalized by the fine portrayal of Alissa Koonen, rare in plasticity and expressiveness. Audiences were stunned by her performance of the soliloquy, "The hall was glittering . . .," its expressive power made even greater by the music.

In one of the composer's letters of 1936, remarkable lines can be found: "You want to know what I'm writing? *The Queen of Spades, Eugene Onegin, Boris Godunov*, and *Mozart and Salieri*. Doesn't it sound like a madman's delirium? But it's true – and the occasion for this is Pushkin's 100th anniversary."

The approaching jubilee of the poet gave Prokofiev a heartening opportunity to encounter the heroes of his best-loved works, to interpret Pushkin's immortal poetry in his own way through his music. The composer wrote the music for M. Romm's film *The Queen of Spades*, for the theatre production of *Boris Godunov* that Vsevolod Meyerhold was preparing, and for the stage version of *Eugene Onegin* at the Kamerny Theatre. Working on *Eugene Onegin* was especially exciting. Prokofiev had always wanted to write an opera based on a Pushkin story; while studying at the Conservatory, he was thinking over a musical interpretation of those parts of the novel not included in

At an anniversary matinee at the Moscow Chamber Theatre. (Left to right): Alexander Tairov, Paul Robeson, Alissa Koonen, Sergei Prokofiev (1934).

Tchaikovsky's opera. He wrote in the *Vechernyaya Moskva* of June 22, 1936: "I think it will be quite interesting to see on stage Lensky and Onegin arguing eagerly over a bottle of good wine, Tatyana visiting Onegin's empty house, or Onegin on the banks of the Neva." Unfortunately, none of the productions based on Pushkin's works was released; but the extraordinary melodic richness of the three scores made it possible for Prokofiev to use themes from these compositions in his later works, *War and Peace, Cinderella, Semyon Kotko*, Symphony No. 7.

In the same years, Prokofiev met again, after a long separation, the friends of his youth. Vera Vladimirovna Alpers, his former fellow-student at the Conservatory, showed him the diaries she kept in her student years. Sincere, moving, truthful, they possibly gave him the idea of writing the *Autobiography*. She also suggested that Prokofiev should write a series of piano pieces for children. The composer initially refused, but a year later he took up this project, an entirely new one for him, and wrote *Children's Music*—a cycle of twelve pieces, poetic and inventive in the style of piano setting.

The symphonic tale *Peter and the Wolf* was another composition for children, "a gift not only to all the children of Moscow, but to my own as well," the composer would say playfully. This idea was given to him by Natalia Ilyinichna Satz, director and artistic administrator of the Children's Theatre, a fervent enthusiast of art education who, from her youth, had devoted herself, commissioned by A. V. Lunacharsky, to work with children. The idea of a merry show with alternation of music and lively, entertaining narrative, with each character represented by the timbre of a specific instrument, seemed quite exciting to Sergei Sergeievich, and he completed the tale in four days. Displayed in the text are the laconic quality of his literary style, the concrete shaping of characters, and Prokofiev's wonderful brand of humor. One can not help smiling when reading the author's manuscript of the text, written in Prokofiev's quaint manner—almost without vowels. One can almost see the famous composer at his desk, with piles of music and very important papers, diligently writing: *"And whn one listened carflly, one culd hear th Duck quackng in th Wolf's blly, bcse th Wolf ws in sch a hrry he swallwed her alive."*

The witty, mirthful music of *Peter and the Wolf* also has a pedagogical function, demonstrating the way particular orchestra instruments sound. Here, Prokofiev strives to achieve explicit contrasts: ". . . Wolf–bird, good–evil, big–small". The strong individuality of characters is parallelled by the sharpness of musical timbres; each character has his own leitmotif.

All the heroes of the tale are very much alive, very vividly depicted. Peter (Petya), the courageous, resolute Young Pioneer, is represented by a string quartet: "He is the many-sided one, after all," Prokofiev explained. The grumbling but good-natured Grandfather (in whose theme one perceives hints at a heroic past!) is characterized by a bassoon. The graceful Cat is a clarinet staccato in the bass register, the fluttering, chirping Bird is a

Prokofiev plays *Peter and the Wolf* to an audience of children at the Central Children's Theatre of Moscow, with Natalia Satz (right) reading the text.

All in the family.

The composer absorbed in one of
his favorite pastimes—playing
chess.

Outstanding actress Alissa Koonen as Cleopatra in *The Egyptian Nights*.

**N. Dolgushin as Boris in the ballet
choreographed by N. Boyarchikov
to Prokofiev's *Boris Godunov*
music.**

flute tune. The Hunters shoot at the wolf "with" timpani and bass drum. The formidable forest-prowler appears to the sounds of three French horns.

Prokofiev found precisely the right tone, warm and trusting, for addressing the youngsters—that was confirmed by hundreds of little listeners in moving letters. A ten-year-old schoolboy wrote: "I really liked the music about Peter, the Bird and the Wolf. When I listened, I recognized everybody. The Cat was pretty, she walked so that no one could hear, she was cunning. The Duck was a silly waddling thing. I was sorry when the Wolf got her. I was glad when I heard her voice in the end. What I liked most was how Peter fought the Wolf, and how all the instruments were playing when the Wolf was caught and they were taking him to the Zoo. I drew a picture of that. I also played the tune on the piano. But it's much more interesting when the orchestra plays it. Please write to me about your next concert."

Soon, the tale became perhaps Prokofiev's most widely performed composition. It brought to adults and children all over the world the joy of acquaintance with the world of symphony music. The merry tale of Peter who outsmarted the Wolf was narrated to audiences by Gérard Philippe, Vera Maretzky, Eleanor Roosevelt . . .

Prokofiev, who had been deprived of direct contact with audiences abroad, discovered, in his native country, the joy of communication with listeners. In his articles, he willingly shared his thoughts on music already written, as well as his creative projects. His writings, lively and easy to understand, were always of an instructive, educational quality, whether he wrote for "adult" papers and magazines, or answered a tricky question from a child in *Pioneer* magazine: "Can melodies ever be exhausted?"

The composer marveled at the interest Soviet audiences take in serious music. Prokofiev called on his colleagues to support this enthusiasm of the general public for genuine, great art, to avoid primitivism—what he termed "sneaking into the coffins of dead composers" and "winking at the audience." Widely known is a 1937 entry in his notebook: "The time is past when music was written for a small circle of aesthetes. Now, great masses of people have, for the first time, faced serious music, and are waiting inquiringly. Composers, pay great attention to this moment: if you repel these crowds, they will go away . . . to things like 'Marussya has taken poison, in the mortuary she lies' (a popular street tune); but, if you hold them, you'll have an audience no one has ever had before . . ."

For several years, Prokofiev searched persistently for a subject for a large scenic work. Even in the years of his life abroad, he asked his friends in the U.S.S.R. to send him books by Soviet authors: "Maybe you'll send me Leonov's *A Hundred* and some other novel . . ." In 1933-1934 he often consulted those whose judgment he respected—Asafiev, Meyerhold. And, finally, after a long search, in late December 1934 Prokofiev's new friend Adrian Piotrovsky, a distinguished man of letters, an expert on theatre and cinema, suggested Shakespeare's *Romeo and Juliet*—a

Manuscript of Prokofiev's original plan for *Romeo and Juliet*.

subject that the composer, to quote his own words, "immediately grasped." Having signed a contract with the Bolshoi Theatre, Sergei Sergeievich went to the Polenovo Rest Resort and set to work on the ballet. In the window of his little house, he could see the quiet Oka, with water-meadows along the gently sloping banks, surrounded by hushed, fairy-tale-like beautiful forests. *Romeo* was completed in the summer of 1935.

In autumn, ballet dancers, choreographers, conductors gathered in the Beethoven hall of the Bolshoi Theatre. Prokofiev played his new ballet. "As he played, the number of listeners grew smaller and smaller. Most of them did not understand Prokofiev's music. They said dancing to such music was unthinkable . . ." Strangely enough, this attitude to the new ballet, described by conductor Yu. Fayer, was shared by many musicians. The masterpiece of modern ballet music was to win recognition among listeners in the form of short gracious suites, performed in concert halls and broadcast on the radio.

The stage premiere of *Romeo and Juliet* in the Kirov Theatre (1940) cost the composer, as well as the producer and the actors, much hard effort. Galina Ulanova recalls in her memoirs how unusual and new that music was, with the metric pulse hard to discern, almost disappearing at times. Arguments would often break out during the rehearsals. The composer, who always firmly defended his author's rights, sometimes agreed to alter the music, to make it more "dance-like." But all the effort was rewarded at the premiere, which won the admiration of both the audience and the press. The young heroine, played by Ulanova, a character so full of light and spirit, and yet so tragic, moved the audience to tears. Juliet became Ulanova's best-loved role.

Of all the many musical interpretations of Shakespeare's *Romeo and Juliet*, it is scarcely possible to name one (except, perhaps, for H. Berlioz's dramatic symphony and P. I. Tchaikovsky's overture-fantasy) that communicates the passion and pathos of the immortal tragedy with as much power and expressiveness. Prokofiev brought to the ballet stage Shakespeare's passionate love of life, his striking humaneness, his stern truthfulness and his slightly crude plebeian humor. It was not only subtlety and accuracy of psychological detail that made Shakespeare so dear to Prokofiev, not only the power of tragic spirit, but also the sharpness of contrasts, the many-sided complexity of images and characters.

At the center of the ballet-tragedy are "the star-crossed lovers." The leading role belongs to Juliet. All of the composer's affection, love, admiration seem to have gone to her. In his music, the young Italian girl changes from a playful, naughty little creature into a tragic, powerful heroine. Now we see her with her nurse before the feast—a restless frolicsome child. Now we see her dancing at the feast with Paris, her future groom; she is all obedience, all submissiveness. Her movements, as outlined by Prokofiev's music, are precise, well-learned, slightly automatic, but not without grace. Now Juliet decides to take the only way Friar Laurence can point to her, and drinks the potion. Fear, terrible premonitions, love that gives her the strength to face the

Alexei Yermolaev as Tybalt.

Sergei Koren in his unforgettable role as Mercutio, the essential Renaissance man with his sparkling love of life.

Galina Ulanova as Juliet. "She is," Prokofiev wrote, "the genius of Russian ballet, its elusive soul, its inspired poetry."

frightening ordeal are expressed in a superbly convincing way. The musical themes given to the young Veronese lovers, especially the love themes, are the best in Prokofiev's lyrical heritage. They are full of sincerity and tenderness, impulse and passion, hope and despair.

The love scenes in *Romeo* are the ones that reveal the extraordinary richness of Prokofiev's melodic genius. His uninhibited, intricate melodies now flow unhurriedly and smoothly, now, as if breaking free of the thick chromatic lace of chords, soar upward and then melt in a soft downward movement. The sudden tonal shifts create an expressive, colorful play of light and dark, and the melody breathes and glitters . . .

Prokofiev's ballet would not be truly Shakespearean without Mercutio. The hero is one bone and one flesh with the merry crowd in the streets of Verona, and is their favorite. A witty, inventive mocker, he is proud and honest. Mercutio's main musical theme is superb, with its sudden, frolicking, capricious leaps and accents. Mercutio jeers at someone cheerfully, thinks up another prank, makes witty jokes. The hero's death in the sunny street, before the eyes of a crowd, is absurd and horrible. Mortally wounded by Tybalt, Mercutio faces death fearlessly, even attempting to turn it all into a joke. Over and over again, the orchestra repeats the Mercutio theme, now broken and wistful, as if struck down in flight. It attempts to rise and whirl around happily, as before. Mercutio's death is cruel and absurd, and Romeo's challenge to Tybalt is inevitable; he avenges his friend's death there, in the square, over his body.

The mass scenes of the ballet are wonderful: temperament and energy in the merriment of the crowd in the street; primness, rather stiff grace in the dances of the nobility at the Capulets' feast; cold elegance in the rather slow dance of the maidens with lilies at the bed of the sleeping Juliet.

Prokofiev finds laconic but strikingly expressive means to depict minor characters—the affectionate, fussing old Nurse, the noble and majestic Friar Laurence. In their delineations, the composer shows his remarkable ability to create the whole of a character with such details as gestures, gait, movement.

Today, *Romeo and Juliet* is one of the most widely performed ballets all over the world. Soon after the premiere, the magnificent beauty, the great power and the full-blooded energy of the music became evident to everyone. The daring, seemingly unthinkable idea—to bring Shakespeare's tragedy to the ballet stage —was realized in a work of highest artistic quality.

In 1937, the country was celebrating the 20th anniversary of the October Revolution. Prokofiev, like other Soviet composers, was eager to meet the anniversary with new compositions worthy of the occasion. The largest of them was the *Cantata for the Twentieth Anniversary of the October Revolution*, the subject of which he defined as: "The Great October Socialist Revolution, the victory, the industrialization of the country, the Constitution."

The idea was a natural one for him. Prokofiev always strove to create images of renewal, of relentless movement forward. Thus

Galina Ulanova as Juliet, Mikhail Gabovich as Romeo.

were born the primeval gusts of the incantation *They Are Seven*, the somewhat schematic pictures of new life in the ballet *The Step Of Steel*; the same impulse shaped the artistic forms of Prokofiev's new civic declaration.

The score of the *Cantata* (almost 250 pages) and the body of performers are astoundingly large-scale. The composition is performed by two choruses—a professional one and an amateur one; by four orchestras—a symphony orchestra, a wind orchestra, an orchestra creating the non-musical background of sound, and an accordion band. The *October Cantata* develops as a series of striking musical tableaux—now lyrical, now full of dynamics of action. From the first episode, with its chaotic storms, with gloomy orchestra sonorities, the development moves towards the central, sixth number ("The Revolution"), a picture of the October insurrection in Petrograd, and then towards the exalted, triumphant finale. The music of the *Cantata* reveals the rapid development of the composer's mastery in solving the most complicated artistic tasks.

In 1938, Prokofiev made his last concert tour abroad—France, Czechoslovakia, England, the U.S.A., crossing the Atlantic on board the enormous French oceanliner "Normandie." The tour through U.S. cities was a brilliant triumph, each appearance, each recital a great success. A Prokofiev Society was formed. While in Los Angeles, he met Austrian theorist and composer Arnold Schoenberg, who emigrated from Germany after Hitler's putsch and was teaching at the Los Angeles University; in Hollywood, he was introduced to Walt Disney (who paid tribute to his work in a screen version of *Peter and the Wolf*). Director R. Mamoulian organized a banquet honoring the Soviet composer; the most famous stars attended—Mary Pickford, Marlene Dietrich, Gloria Swanson, Douglas Fairbanks.

On his return home, Prokofiev fervently went to work at new compositions, among them music for the film *Alexander Nevsky*.

In his busy and eventful life as an artist, Prokofiev met many talented people. His meeting with Sergei Eisenstein was one of the happy encounters fortune granted him. In the very first days of their acquaintance in France, where Eisenstein was on assignment with director G. Alexandrov and shooting operator E. Tisse, Prokofiev was enchanted by the breadth and scope of this extraordinary man's talent, by his powerful imperious charisma. "I wish we could work together!" he thought at that time.

In 1938, the wish to "work together" was fulfilled: Eisenstein was filming *Alexander Nevsky*. Prokofiev enthusiastically watched him work, admired the inventiveness of the filming group. The thrill of participation in the birth of the film about the Russian people's victory over the fierce Teutonic crusaders carried everybody away. A year before World War II started, the prophetic words of the Novgorod prince and general Alexander Yaroslavich came from the screen: "Whoever comes to us with a sword will die by the sword. This is and will be the stronghold of the Russian land."

Prokofiev worked selflessly. Eisenstein later recalled how it was:

Manuscript of the first page of the *Cantata for the Twentieth Anniversary of the October Revolution*. "I wrote this cantata with great enthusiasm. The complex events of which it speaks required a complexity of musical language. But I hope that the passion and the sincerity of this music will make it accessible to our audiences."

" 'You'll have the music by 12 noon.'

"We leave the small screening room. And, even though it's midnight, I am not worried at all. At 11:55 exactly, a small dark blue car will enter the gates of the studio.

"From that car, Sergei Prokofiev will emerge, holding the new musical piece for *Alexander Nevsky*.

"We screen the new film episode at night.

"In the morning, we'll have the new piece of music for it."

The result of the collaboration of Eisenstein and Prokofiev in the creation of *Alexander Nevsky* is unique. The music is the active dynamic force of the film. The rhythm of movement in the frame, its accents, the dynamics of the emotional structure of images seem to be born simultaneously with Prokofiev's music. Having seen an episode several times, he would grasp all the particular details, so that he could, to quote Eisenstein, "on the next day recreate the musical equivalent of the image in the musical score." The director revered the composer's zeal and returned it on his part. One can hardly name another instance in filmmaking of a director shooting —or re-shooting—scenes to a sound-track ready in advance. In the 30s, and later, too, it was quite out of the ordinary.

Eisenstein pointed out accurately and graphically one of the aspects of Prokofiev's talent: "His place is not with sets, illusory landscapes and 'the breathtaking slope of the stage,' but, more than anywhere, in the midst of microphones, flashes of photo-cells, with the celluloid spiral of film, the unerring precision of the movement of the camera's cogwheels, the exactness, the synchronism, the mathematical accuracy of the length and footage of the film . . ." The semi-fantastic atmosphere of cinematography could have been created for Prokofiev's inventive, incredibly imaginative, and yet extremely precise mind.

Prokofiev working with Sergei Eisenstein.

The mood-texture of *Alexander Nevsky*, as conceived by the composer, is divided in two spheres—the Russian and the Teutonic; the music characterizing the enemy force was to sound "grating to the Russian ear." The effect of the dull mechanistic march of the "dog-knights," of sinister, frightening harmonic superimpositions, was increased with the help of new sound-recording means Prokofiev discovered. He tried various ways of arranging orchestra groups before the microphones, regulating the balance of timbres from the recording room. Sound operator B. Volsky recalled that Prokofiev experimented with instruments before the microphone, trying to distort the sound, "to make it disagreeable, and so that one couldn't tell what the instrument was." The "upside-down" orchestration Prokofiev invented, with loud instruments placed far from the microphone, and the soft ones close to it, had quite a curious effect. What came out was a "big," "formidable" oboe and a "small" trumpet.

The film was first screened on December 1, 1938. The brilliant team that included, besides Eisenstein and Prokofiev, operator E. Tisse, actors N. Cherkassov, N. Okhlopkov, V. Massalitinova, A. Abrikossov, created a film that almost instantly won great popularity and love with audiences. More and more copies of the film were in constant demand.

In the late spring of 1939, Prokofiev conducted the cantata *Alexander Nevsky*, based on the music of the film. The clarity of the setting of the seven-part composition is a result of the logicalness of the construction and the rapid dynamics of the development of contrasting "frame" images.

The sadness and pain of serfdom are expressed in the first part of the cantata, "Russia Under Mongolian Subjugation." Prokofiev laconically presents a picture of torn and bleeding Russia. The next two pieces, "The Song of Alexander Nevsky" and "The Crusaders in Pskov," are an exposition of two conflicting powers. Here, one feels the distinct, striking contrast between the mood-structures of the Russian and the Teutonic spheres that Prokofiev wanted to achieve. At first, they are set apart, to reveal all their incompatibility at the culmination point, in "The Battle on Ice." The crusaders are a brutal grim force, with an unthinking determination to go forward, to conquer new lands. That is why they appear so sinister, so ugly, so inhuman; that is why the unique, extraordinary means Prokofiev found after a long search are so natural. Russian warriors go forth to meet the enemy powers, proudly and joyously conscious of the rightness of their cause. That is why the upbeat, heroic character of their themes — song-like or recklessly merry and dance-like — comes so naturally.

"The Song of Alexander Nevsky" is a manly chorus with a melody majestic in its unaffected simplicity. The enemy force ("The Crusaders in Pskov") is monstrous and multi-faceted. The harsh dissonances of brass give way to a hypocritically pious choral. In the middle of the piece, we hear a wailing complaint of the strings — the lament of the Pskovians taken prisoner.

The music of part four is a call to combat. The Russian troops get ready for the decisive battle. The heroic pitch of the chorus, "Rise up, O Russian people," was especially remarkable even on the eve of the Soviet people's fight for their land against those whom Eisenstein called "the loathsome descendants" of the Teutonic knights.

The eventful, action-filled part of the composition is concentrated in the next episode ("The Battle on Ice"). On the ice of the Chudskoye lake, two incompatible forces clash, and the destiny of the world depends on the outcome ... Here, Prokofiev's music is graphic in the best sense of the word. It has the crow's cawing in it, the quivering of hazy air before dawn, the crack of the breaking ice ... Diverse in material, as if pieced together from little sonorous "frames," the musical picture develops in a strictly organized way. The mechanistic march and the lifeless singing of the crusaders alternate with the Russian themes, the heroic call from the song "Rise Up, O Russian People," with the buffoons' playful tunes. Suddenly, the "Russian counter-attack" theme bursts in like shining light. The Russian cavalry tears forward to meet the spear-bristled Teutonic monster ...

After the scope and the decorative richness of color of "The Battle on Ice" comes the unforgettable lyricism of part six, called "The Dead Field." A stately Russian beauty with long tresses walks around the battlefield at night, torch in hand, looking for

A frame from the movie *Alexander Nevsky*.

her fiance among the dead. The noble shapes of the truly Russian song-like, austere melody express the restrained sorrow of all the Russian people.

In the finale of the cantata ("Alexander Enters Pskov") the composer brings together the Russian themes of the composition. "The Song of Alexander Nevsky" flows, hymn-like, and the victorious chime of church-bells joins in. The cantata ends with a monumental picture of the holy triumph of the Russian people.

Shortly after the cantata was completed, Prokofiev set about to realize a project he conceived long ago — an opera on a Soviet subject. As early as 1933, he wrote in an article published by the *Sovetskaya Muzika (Soviet Music)* magazine: "I have a great desire to write an opera with a Soviet theme, but it's not so easy to find a suitable libretto . . ." And, finally, he found one. Writer Alexey Tolstoy advised him to read V. Katayev's recently published short novel, *I Am a Son of the Working People.*

The composer found many interesting themes in the book: ". . . There are the young and their love, those who belong to the old world and their hatred; the heroism of struggle, tears for losses, and merry jests so characteristic of Ukrainian humor. Katayev's characters are absolutely alive, and that is the most important thing. They live, they are happy or angry, they laugh — and it is this life I wanted to show when I chose Katayev's novel for the opera *Semyon Kotko*."

(From *Semyon Kotko*) Elena Obraztsova as Frosya, A. Arkhipov as Mikola.

A peaceful Ukrainian village lives its ordinary quiet life. Soldier Semyon comes back from the front, exuberantly happy to see his mother, his fiancee Sophya, the friendly villagers. The sudden invasion of the German troop breaks, ruins the life of the village. Merry sailor Tzaryov is executed, his fiancee Liubka goes mad, and Mikola, a pathetic, funny adolescent boy, kills a German sentinel in a critical situation and becomes a true avenger.

Prokofiev, who worked on the opera with great enthusiasm, wanted, above all, the characters, actions and language of the heroes to be true to life and to his artistic beliefs. "I don't need any arias or poetry," he argued with Katayev, who expected the opera to be filled with songs and dancing. Dialogue, recitative, "slice-of-life" sketches predominate in the opera. Its dynamics are quite special, for its structure revolves around rapidly interchanging "microforms" — short ariosos, dialogues, even separate phrases. Their natural development creates the impression of a changeful flow of life, rich in nuances and contrasts. In no other opera of his, perhaps, did Prokofiev show so mature a mastery of striking, realistic character portrayal. Brilliantly successful, for instance, was the character of Frossya, Semyon's high-spirited fourteen-year-old sister. The energetic girl is active and enterprising, she is always at the center of everything that is going on. Frossya "chatters" with Semyon and Sophya, confidently advising her confused brother on the matchmakers he ought to send to Sophya's father to ask her in marriage. Remaining alone, she suddenly becomes pensive and slightly wistful, humming her song, "There's a noise, there's a rumble . . ."

Colorful Ukrainian colloquialisms are easily recognizable in the characters' speech. The short word "Mutually," the greetings Semyon, on his return to his native village, exchanges with the peasants who gather around his hut, sound solemn and "dignified." Sophya, talking to Semyon coquettishly, repeats the same words several times: "And now, I say, good-bye to you." This short, one-time phrase reveals the girl's tender grace, the gentleness of her nature, the elegance of her gestures.

It is the truth of real life that dictates all the particular details of the opera. The matchmakers sent by Semyon go to the Tkachenkos' house. Sophya, excited and quite confused, and her mother Khivrya get ready to go out and meet the matchmakers. In the next room, former *kulak* (wealthy peasant) Tkachenko, who hates both Semyon and his messengers, sailor Tzaryov and Selsoviet (village council) chairman Remenyuk, talks to them composedly. Prokofiev was thrilled by this scene of two parallel lines of action developing simultaneously; he even made a drawing of the characters' positions on the stage. The realism of the opera is evident in the way the composer drastically and radically changes the atmosphere set in the beginning. In the middle of the third act, the lyrical story colored with lively folk humor suddenly gives way to high, exalted tragedy. Tender and loving Liubka becomes the spokeswoman for the mass of the people, for the sorrow of all Ukrainians. Her mad, desperate exclamations form a tremendous ostinato—a short descending motive is repeated many times, strengthened by chorus and orchestra. German troops are approaching, Tkachenko fusses around in his house, getting ready to receive the German commander, Semyon and Mikola flee to the steppe, taking the bodies of their executed comrades with them, the Germans come and set Semyon's hut on fire, the alarm-bell strikes, and Liubka, no longer aware of what is happening, frenziedly repeats a motive that seems to hover over the other heroes' voices.

Prokofiev wanted his opera to be produced by Meyerhold in the Stanislavsky Theatre. But this was never achieved and instead, Serafima Birman was appointed producer of the opera. An exceptionally gifted actress, she was instantly thrilled by the new work—on the very day that Prokofiev sang and played the opera to her, in a room at the Kislovodsk health resort. At the rehearsals of the opera, two commanding, fiery temperaments clashed: the composer's and the producer's. Preparations for the premiere were stormy and tumultuous. Sergei Sergeievich kept intervening persistently in the stage action, demonstrating how the actors should move and gesticulate, how Semyon should knock at the window of his hut and then wait for his knock to be returned . . .

At the premiere, opinions were divided. As often happened, many were puzzled by the novelty of Prokofiev's new work. The captious composer himself was not quite satisfied with the production, but there were many enthusiastic, eager admirers of *Semyon Kotko*. Their response seems to have anticipated the rebirth of Prokofiev's masterpiece in the 1960s. Among the young enthusiasts was Conservatory student Svyatoslav Richter: "The night I heard *Semyon Kotko*, I realized Prokofiev was a

A scene from *Semyon Kotko*.

Prokofiev in the late 1930s.

World-famous Russian pianist
Svyatoslav Richter.

great composer." The production of *Semyon Kotko* raised a heated discussion. A series of articles with most controversial evaluations of the new opera was printed in the *Sovetskaya Muzika* magazine.

The arguments which the composer's work stirred up were not to quiet down for years. They were to last; the new ways Prokofiev presented were not adaptable to everyone, for his art was too complex, too many-faceted, too extraordinary. However, both those who gave his talent its due and those who failed to understand his music at first, felt its tremendous power, the great power of its creator's personality. The impression Prokofiev made on those around him was imprinted on their memory for years. Grave, collected, he was exceedingly businesslike and strict, often captious, wherever his work, his creativity, or music in general was concerned. He reprimanded eighteen-year-old Oistrakh at the concert, before a full audience, for a performance of the scherzo from Concerto No. 1 that didn't please him. He was quite harsh on a woman poet who had written an unsatisfactory text for *Peter and the Wolf*. Serafima Birman could not help mentioning his "unjust fault-finding" in her memoirs. "What you need is drums, not music!" he told Galina Ulanova. Yet, exacting as he was of others, the basic reason for that was his relentless exigency towards himself.

He worked with dedication and with a rare punctuality. Often, he returned to works already completed, to make alterations. Having decided to write an autobiographical sketch, he worked at it scrupulously, heeding the editor's advice.

Another quality, too, reveals the flamboyancy and complexity of his individuality: he is never the same. In his powerful piano technique, he is outwardly subdued and calm. When he mounts the podium, "his whole being begins to gesticulate" (S. Moreux). His austerity, sometimes verging on dryness and arrogance in dealing with other people, gives way suddenly to good-natured gentleness, the ability to laugh merrily and infectiously, to make jokes, to be playful. His appearance was quite peculiar, too. A high, noble brow, a slim, straight nose with a fold at the bridge, between the closely knit eyebrows, a boyishly large mouth, chubby cheeks, clear, childish blue eyes, a good-natured, even a little helpless, smile. Richter described the unforgettable impression that his appearance made:

"Once, on a sunny day, I was walking along the Arbat and saw an unusual man. There was an air of defiant power about him; he passed by me like a phenomenon. His boots were bright yellow, his suit checked, his tie orange-red.

"I couldn't help turning and following him with my eyes—it was Prokofiev."

After *Semyon Kotko*, Prokofiev suddenly became interested in a very different subject. The young poet Myra Mendelson was working on a translation of *Duenna*, a comedy by the English playwright Sheridan, and offered it to the composer as a libretto. Sergei Sergeievich was delighted: "Why, this is champagne, this can make an opera in the Mozart or Rossini style!" Together

A scene from *Semyon Kotko*.

with M. Mendelson (after Prokofiev's divorce from Lina Llubera, she became his wife and his full-time collaborator) he prepared the stage script and the libretto for the future lyric-comic opera.

At that time, a brilliant MKHAT (Moscow Academic Art Theatre) production of Sheridan's *School for Scandal* with the leading trio of Olga Androvsky, Mikhail Yanshin and Anatoly Ktorov, was a great success in Moscow. Prokofiev was certainly familiar with this performance; at any rate, he mentioned it in his short essay about his work on the opera. About the comedy Prokofiev wrote: "I was fascinated by the fine wit, the enchanting lyricism, the astute characterization of the *dramatis personae,* the dynamics of actions, the attention-holding construction of the plot, so enthralling that each new turn is awaited impatiently."

The experiment with *The Duenna* (the composer entitled his opera *Betrothal in a Nunnery*) is another proof of Prokofiev's flexible, unprejudiced approach to any artistic task. *Semyon Kotko*, the opera he had just completed, demonstrated the validity and the wide possibilities of through-composed construction of opera, almost without rounded arias, songs or ensembles. An opera after Sheridan, on the other hand, presupposed both through-composed musical development and pieces complete in themselves. In the comedies of the "English Beaumarchais," the element of music is usually very important—for instance, in *School for Scandal*, one of Sir Peter's numerous brawls with his wife is accompanied by an idyllic duet of a flute and a harp. In *The Duenna*, Prokofiev renders, in a marvellously humorous way, the music-making scene in Scene 6.

The richness of the opera's glistening colors is overwhelming. It organically combines merry comedy and delicate lyricism. The development of the plot is rapid, non-stop. Comic elements are mixed with the passionate effusions of Louisa and Antonio, Clara and Ferdinand declaring their love. Just as in the earlier opera, *Love For Three Oranges*, festive merriment invades the performance imperiously. Mischievous carnival masks tease angry Don Jerome, interrupt Antonio's serenade with their whirling dance in the end of Scene 1; the noisy carnival atmosphere seems to light up everything that happens on the stage, like a magic lantern.

Greedy Don Jerome and aging womanizer Mendoza are the comic characters of the opera. They are portrayed in a sharply satirical way. Mendoza is pompous, cunning, sharp-witted. He chatters excitedly with Don Jerome, thrilled by the prospect of marriage to young pretty Louisa. He is very well characterized by the often-repeated cues: voluptuously ecstatic ("Oh, that sly little thing!") or clumsily smug ("Oh, what a smart boy Mendoza is!"). Greedy, grumbling Don Jerome is a descendant of Don Bartolo from Rossini's *The Barber of Seville*. He wants to arrange a profitable marriage for his daughter and is willing to exchange her beauty for the disgusting Mendoza's ducats. Don Jerome fawns enthusiastically on his future son-in-law, rapturously describing Louisa's merits, and then, when he is alone, com-

An illustration to the program of *Betrothal in a Nunnery* at the Berlin Staatsoper (1959).

**Sergei Prokofiev with his second
wife, poet Myra Mendelson.**

E. Maximenko as Mendoza, T.
Yanko as the Duenna. "When one
listens to *The Duenna*, one
remembers Verdi's *Falstaff* - the
same spontaneity of feeling
enriched by the wisdom of a great
master." *(Dmitry Shostakovich)*

A. Khalileyeva as Louisa.

V. Ulyanov as Don Jerome in *Betrothal in a Nunnery.*

plains: "If you have a daughter, believe me, it's a plague."

"When I set to work on an opera based on *The Duenna,* I had two ways to choose from: the first, to emphasize in my music the comic side of the play; the second, to emphasize the lyricism. It was the second that I chose." The two young, passionately loving couples are the heroes of Prokofiev's opera. While in *Love for Three Oranges* the ecstatic outbursts of the suddenly cured Prince were viewed with some ironic mockery, in his next comic opera, almost ten years later, the author felt sincere, emotional sympathy for the young lovers. The music of the lyrical episodes is warm, beautiful, harmonious. Such is Antonio's delightful serenade in Act I; the melody will reappear in Act III, in the duet to which happy Louisa and Antonio go to their wedding. The thoughtful, sad mood of Clara who has been sent to a nunnery (Act III) is accompanied by graceful, harmonious music. Even Mendoza is drawn in the exalted lyrical quartet in Act III. The bright mood of this fragment is especially impressive when set against the next episode of domestic music-making at Don Jerome's.

An amusing trio is on the stage. Don Jerome rapturously draws musical passages out of a clarinet; his friend is absorbed in playing his cornet-à-piston; and Sancho, the butler, beats a big drum very diligently, often falling out of rhythm . . .

The wonderful qualities of *Betrothal in a Nunnery*—its life-celebrating exuberance, the fineness of its musical style—remained unknown to audiences for a long time. The war began, and work on the production was interrupted. It was only in 1946 that the premiere at the S. M. Kirov Opera and Ballet Theatre in Leningrad introduced this opera, one of Prokofiev's most popular, to the stage.

A scene from *Betrothal in a Nunnery*.

On the eve of the war, the music lovers of the country were celebrating two remarkable anniversaries: Prokofiev's fiftieth (April 23) and Myaskovsky's sixtieth (April 20). At the request of *Sovetskaya Muzika* magazine, the two composers posed for a picture. The camera preserved Myaskovsky's kind, tired look, with Prokofiev at his side smiling and full of energy. In April 1941, one could hardly foresee that the twelve years of life he had left would be filled not only with fruitful work and the creation of beautiful music, but also with anxiety, suffering, struggle. Ahead were war, evacuation, and, in the year of Victory, the first attack of the incurable illness that tormented him for the rest of his life. And now, he had plans, exciting plans, and no ordeal could stop him from going forward, towards new achievement.

"Victorious Forever"

The Great Patriotic war made all Soviet men and women draw on all the moral and physical strength they had, dedicate all of their energy, work and talent to the cause of victory. Those who were going to the front and those who were staying behind fought against fascist Germany, defending not only the independence of their country, the life and liberty of their children, but the best of what humanity had created.

From the very first days of the war, Prokofiev changed his plans drastically. He interrupted his work on the ballet *Cinderella* and on the production of *The Duenna*. The warriors of the Red Army who were fighting the enemy needed songs—valorous songs that call to battle, and also warm and lyrical ones, songs that make one think of going home, of the peaceful life that will come after the victory. The composer's immediate response to the events of the first months of the war was to set to music V. Mayakovsky's "The Admiral Riff-raff," A. Surkov's "The Song of the Brave," five poems by Myra Mendelson ("The Tankman's Oath," "The Son of Kabarda" (an area in Georgia, in the south of the U.S.S.R), "The Warrior's Sweetheart," "Fritz," "The Warrior's Love").

Prokofiev working with Myra Mendelson-Prokofieva.

At first, the Prokofievs stayed not far from Moscow, in Kratovo. "Even though that country place was not a target for attacks, enemy airplanes often shrieked over our heads at night, throwing star-shells to find their way . . . Bright white rays of search-lights crossed the sky. These search-lights, the fighter-planes leaving shining traces of green behind them, the yellow illuminating 'lamps' the Germans sent down created a sight of sinister beauty."

The shattering experiences of the first war months were reflected in the symphonic suite *1941*. It consists of three short parts—"The Battle," "At Night," "For the Brotherhood of Nations." The composer explained their contents: "The first is a picture of heated combat, experienced by the listener now as if from a distance, now as if he were on the battlefield; the second is a picture of poetic night invaded by the tension of approaching action; the third, a solemn and lyrical hymn to victory and to the brotherhood of nations."

In August, Prokofiev and his family moved to the Caucasus, to Nalchik, where he shared the hardships of evacuation with many

Prokofiev and Myaskovsky in 1941.

The famous "Ivan at Anastasia's bier" scene from *Ivan the Terrible*, with Nikolai Cherkassov as Ivan.

outstanding artists, including N. Myaskovsky, Yu. Shaporin, A. Goldenveiser, O. Knipper-Chekhova, V. Nemirovich-Danchenko, I. Grabar. Together with his colleagues, he participated in concerts at the local theatre, performed at hospitals for recuperating soldiers, explored the riches of local folklore. There, in Nalchik, the composer wrote a string quartet based on Kabardian tunes—an original work, brilliantly and faithfully rendering the peculiar qualities of Caucasian folk music.

Those who were close to Sergei Sergeievich in those months witnessed the creation of the first scenes of the opera *War and Peace* on which his attention remained centered for the rest of his life.

In November 1941, when the situation at the front became more complicated, the Prokofievs moved to Tiflis. An unusually cold winter and lack of material comforts did not impede the creative activity of the musicians whose performances enriched the panorama of the Georgian capital's art world. Prokofiev gave recitals, as did K. Igumnov, A. Gauk, S. Feinberg. However, he continued to work every day on his new compositions. At that time, he wrote feverishly, overwhelmed by new ideas he hardly had time to put down on any scrap of paper at hand.

In May 1942, Prokofiev joined Eisenstein in Alma-Ata for collaboration on the film *Ivan the Terrible*. The composer was thrilled by the prospect of working with his friend again: "I am looking forward to our collaboration with great tenderness." He was not set back by the long, hard journey, which he managed to use to work on the orchestration of *War and Peace*, or by the discomforts of life in Alma-Ata: a small hotel room, the occasional disruption of electricity, food shortages. "Prokofiev was active, cheerful, full of plans," G. Ulanova recalls.

At that time, the united motion picture studios of Moscow and Leningrad were at work in the capital of Kazakhstan. Prokofiev wrote music for the movies *Kotovsky* and *Tonya*, worked on the sound-track of *Lermontov*, for which he had written the music earlier, in Tiflis. Eisenstein, who produced *War and Peace* at the Bolshoi, assisted the composer in his work on the opera. Some of his drawings, sketches for episodes of the future production, have been preserved.

In Alma-Ata, Prokofiev and Eisenstein set to work on their second masterpiece—a monumental historical film about Ivan the Terrible. Unlike the clear-cut juxtaposition of forces in *Alexander Nevsky*, there are no black and white characteristics in *Ivan the Terrible*. Complex, controversial characters and images form, by the will of S. Eisenstein, a multi-layered, infinitely complicated structure with inner ramifications. It was not accidental that Serafima Birman, selected for the role of Princess Staritsky, wrote to the director: "Through my character of Efrossinia, I shall carry out, with the utmost dedication and the strictest accuracy, all the notational signs, all the intervals, the sharps and the flats that you, the composer, need in the sound of the symphony you are creating."

It was a symphony-film that Eisenstein envisioned, and, just as before, his vision enthralled, "infected" Prokofiev. Trusting the direc-

One of Eisenstein's sketches Prokofiev used as "cribs" in writing his music for *Ivan the Terrible*.

tor, the composer agreed to write music only by "cribs"—graphic sketches of future shots. The director, trusting the composer, shot some of the scenes to the sound of ready musical fragments.

Prokofiev's music for *Ivan the Terrible* marks another step forward in his growth as a master of national drama and as a tragic composer. The music in mass scenes is monumental in scope. Such, for instance, is the colorful wedding scene, with the traditional bells, the chorus singing "Many Years" (an old Russian church hymn, asking God to grant those for whom it is sung "many years" of happy, prosperous life); the music renders all the characteristic qualities of old church singing. The women's choruses—the song of praise, "Young Oaks Are Growing on the Mountain," and the glorification song, "There Goes a White Swan"—are captivating.

The episode of the Tsar's troops going to war to take the city of Kazan is strikingly picturesque. There is stern power and an almost savage beauty in the gunners' song; the music in the scenes where the city is taken by storm is shockingly ruthless.

Eisenstein wanted the scene of the oprichniks' feast to be the culmination of the film. (The oprichniks: a special "task force" created by Ivan the Terrible to investigate "treason" and crush the disobedient nobility.) On the screen is a youthful force that moves history forward but also brings death and destruction with it. Many years ago, in *Battleship Potemkin*, in the final shot, the director showed the flag in red. In *Ivan the Terrible*, a complex, dense texture of black-and-white—light and dark, sharp contours and fuzzy patches of light, shades, sudden changes—develops to culminate in the blood-red spots of the oprichniks' shirts in the scene of their drunken revel. Both of the oprichniks dances stun the viewer with dashing merriment and sinister strength.

The director, the composer and the leading actor N. Cherkasov were all trying to communicate the tragic complexity of the character of the terrible but suffering Tsar Ivan. The "Ivan at Anastasia's Bier" scene is most expressive. The directing, Cherkasov's acting and the music convey a piercing feeling of loneliness, fear and despair.

In one of the film's most unforgettable moments, Efrossinia Staritsky, freed from the terrible burden of her plot to murder the Tsar, runs happily to the cathedral. She wants to make sure that "the beast is dead," that no obstacle can now prevent her dearly loved son from ascending the throne. But there, on the stone floor, decked in the royal garb, lies her Vladimir, a weak-willed boy who was crowned only to die. Petrified with grief, the Princess sings a lullaby, "Song About the Beaver," to her dead son. The somber expressiveness of the melody, the heartbreaking sorrow emphasized, in the film, by I. Yaunzem's beautiful singing, making a sinister, indelible impression.

In 1946, the creators of the first part of *Ivan the Terrible* (director S. Eisenstein, operator E. Tisse, composer S. Prokofiev, actors S. Cherkasov and S. Birman) were awarded the State Prize. The second part was not released until twelve years later. S. Eisenstein, who looked forward to making a third film about

Prokofiev and Eisenstein working in Alma-Ata.

Ivan, died suddenly in 1948. To all subsequent offers of work for the cinema, Prokofiev invariably replied: "After the death of Sergei Mikhailovich Eisenstein, I consider my work for cinematography finished."

The trip to Moscow, in the autumn of 1942, had to do with projects of performances of his new works. Prokofiev introduced Myaskovsky to the recently written *Ballad of a Boy Who Remained Unknown*, a dramatic cantata to a poem by P. Antokolsky. Young S. Richter, having learned Sonata No. 7 in four days, performed it very successfully at the October Hall of the House of the Unions. In the blacked-out building of the Bolshoi Theatre, in a room lit by two paraffin lampions, the composer played *War and Peace* for S. Samosud and B. Pokrovsky. That was the goal of his trip, the reason for that long and exhausting journey. He was excited and anxious about the planned production. He worked on *War and Peace* for ten more years, perfecting the opera.

Tolstoy and Prokofiev . . . It must have been inevitable that the composer should write a work linked to the prose of the great writer and thinker. *War and Peace* was created at the crossroads of the many tendencies that characterize both the inner creative processes of the growth of the composer's individuality and the historic conditions that prompted the creation of the epic opera. The 1930s and 1940s are the time when Prokofiev reached genuine maturity as an artist. In that period, he achieved a remarkable clarity and purity of perfect, finished style. Patriotism, awareness of an artist's public duty to his country were fortified in him after his return to the Motherland, in the years when the astounded composer was rediscovering Russia—the rapid dynamics of its growth, the day-to-day heroism of its working people, their enthusiastic acceptance of the beauty of art. The ordeals of wartime, the hardships of evacuation, the tragic impressions of war heightened his awareness of his blood bonds to the Motherland. War gave a powerful impetus toward the realization of his idea, conceived in the 30s, of an opera based on *War and Peace*. In prewar art, the trend toward trying to understand the meaning of the present by drawing upon historical subjects became very strong. On the eve of war, work after work was written about the past of the peace-loving, but invincible people—Yu. Shaporin's symphony-cantata *On the Kulikovo Field*, M. Koval's opera and oratorio *Emelyan Pugachov*, Prokofiev's cantata *Alexander Nevsky*. From this point of view, the choice of the novel makes sense, for the processes of spiritual evolution and moral search connected with the events of the 1812 Patriotic War served Tolstoy as one of the means of understanding the reality of his time.

Prokofiev had always loved Tolstoy. Abroad and later, on his return to Russia, he read and re-read the great writer's novels. When, in 1935, in Chelyabinsk on a recital tour, he had a conversation with singer Vera Dukhovskaya about the novel *War and Peace*, he admitted that he "had been thinking, for a long time, of writing an opera on the subject," but kept delaying it, aware that "such a subject requires long and hard work." Shortly before the war, he told Myra Mendelson he envisioned the scene of wound-

The first page of the manuscript of the suite *1941*.

Manuscript of the *Ballad of the Boy Who Remained Unknown.*

ed Prince Andrei's encounter with Natasha as an operatic scene.

The war that began focused his thoughts immediately on the future opera. Later, Prokofiev recalled: "In those days, my vague thoughts about writing an opera based on Tolstoy's novel *War and Peace* took a clear shape. The pages about the Russian people's struggle against Napoleon's troops in 1812, about the retreat of Napoleon's army from the Russian land, became particularly dear to me." In the hard conditions of evacuation in Nalchik, then in Tiflis, Prokofiev wrote, with an obsessive zeal unusual even for him, his best-loved opera, with a libretto by M. Mendelson.

In the lyrical scenes, only the text of the novel was used. However, it was necessary to draw on other literary material for the epic scenes. In her memoirs, M. Mendelson lists collections of Russian folk-songs, proverbs and sayings, as well as the notes of guerilla-fighter and poet Denis Davidov and a guide to the Borodino battle location. In April 1942, the piano-score of the opera's first edition, in eleven scenes, was completed. About a year later, the opera was orchestrated. At the request of the Committee on Art Affairs, and later, in connection with the coming premiere in Leningrad in 1946, Prokofiev continued to work on the opera. On one hand, it was necessary to expand the choral scenes and the finale, to make them more graphic, to emphasize the character of Kutuzov. On S. Samosud's suggestion, Prokofiev composed two more scenes—"Ball at the Place of a Courtier of Empress Catherine" and "Military Council in Fili." At the same time, several episodes of a domestic nature were shortened. In October 1943, rehearsals in the Bolshoi began but it was not until 1959 that the opera was performed on the GABT stage. A concert performance of the opera in the Conservatory Grand Hall was done by S. Samosud. The three concerts in June 1945, and, a year later, the premiere of the first part of the opera at the Maly (Small) Leningrad Opera Theatre (MALEGOT), were a tremendous success and were received as a grandiose hymn to the great victory of the Soviet people.

War and Peace is at the center of Prokofiev's work in the Soviet period. The opera included many musical themes that can be found in his notebooks as early as 1933, fragments from the music for the production of *Eugene Onegin,* for the film *Lermontov.* Besides, the composer used melodies of authentic Cossack songs from A. Listopadov's collection, a melody from his own music for the film *Ivan the Terrible.* He went back to *War and Peace* many times, long after the original version was completed. The last alterations were made as late as 1952. Thus, Prokofiev gave more time to this opera than to any other of his works.

There are a great number of characters in *War and Peace*; the tone of narration is now subdued, now solemn and lofty; fine, delicate writing gives way to large strokes, to massive, thick sonorities. Tolstoy's prose serves as a basis for aria-like, song-like fragments, with melodic pictures of striking sculptural beauty, for recitative close to simple speech, for genre episodes recreating the atmosphere of high-society daily life in the 19th century. Action takes place in the chamber atmosphere of drawing-rooms, in Pierre's study, at the ball—and also, at the battlefield, in burning Moscow, on the Smolensky road. It is flexible and fanciful, just as life itself.

The first part of the opera shows the peaceful life of glittering urban society and ends in the announcement that war has started. The second half (scenes 8 to 13) is devoted to military events. Following Tolstoy, Prokofiev emphasizes the fact that the historic force truly crucial to the outcome of the 1812 war was the Russian people. That is why Kutuzov is not so much an outstanding individual as a general close to the people and loved by the people. That is why his musical characterization is so closely interwoven with the thematic construction of folk scenes.

As always, Prokofiev is brief and laconic in outlining his characters; but the laconic sketches are precise and poetic at the same time. Not only the heroes but even minor characters are given sharply individual characteristics. Making use of vocal declamation, the composer creates unforgettable portraits of stubborn Prince Bolkonsky, seductive Elene, conceited Kuragin, brave coachman Balaga, gypsy girl Matryosha.

Natasha Rostova is one of the best-loved and most charming heroines in Russian literature. What makes her so remarkable is her special, penetrating sense of moral strength and of the beauty of life, the sincerity of her rich nature.

. . . On a lovely moonlit night in Otradnoye, Prince Andrei cannot sleep. The words of the unseen girl who wants to fly away to the sky are so exalted that they stir up "a causeless vernal feeling of joy and renewal" in the soul of Bolkonsky, who has lived through so much. The melody of the flute, with an accompaniment of violins, is tender and mysteriously lovely, as if born from a flow of moonlight. Natasha's sincere and slightly naive utterances give way to her duet with Sonya, "O meandering brook," stylized in the tradition of early 19th century song-lyrics.

In the second scene ("The Ball"), Natasha's fragment, the waltz, is the best musically. Next to the graphic, prosaic characteristics of old Count Rostov, Akhrosimova, Denisov, the waltz appears, like a small poem. The beautiful music renders, with astonishing inspiration, Natasha's chastity and timidity, her airy grace and charm.

The heroine's personality is shown in continuous dynamic development. Now Natasha feels insulted by the uncivil reception at old Bolkonsky's house. Her short arioso is full of annoyance, pain, desire to meet Prince Andrei. The melody moves timidly at first, in a narrow range, and then grows breathtakingly, soaring upwards, lit with a bright, major-mode glow.

We see a very different heroine in scene 6 ("At Akhrosimova's Mansion"). In Tolstoy's novel, the episode of the failed elopement is a crucial one in the development of the character. The sublime and naive ideals of youth are shattered in the encounter with people of "a vicious, heartless breed." In the dialogue with Akhrosimova, Natasha's infinite suffering is rendered through nervous, jerky intonations, accompanied by a short, self-contained motive repeated in the orchestra over and over, like a

Prokofiev and Samuel Samosud at a rehearsal of the concert performance of *War and Peace*. "The long-awaited premiere was, at last, held on June 7, 9 and 11," Samosud reminisced. "Sergei Sergeievich attended, I believe, all three performances. There was an atmosphere of rare celebration in the hall. Even though it was summertime, the performance of *War and Peace* drew practically all the cream of the capital's cultural world, writers, musicians, scientists, military men. Prokofiev got a real ovation. He was greatly moved by such a reception."

tormenting thought unable to find an outlet. In the next scene (the conversation with Pierre), Natasha's part is especially expressive: sorrowful exclamations, phrases faltering sadly, pleas for pardon, interrupted by the shaken girl's sobbing.

Natasha comes to visit wounded Andrei, who is dying in a dark peasant hut in Mytishi. The nervousness of intonations is gone from her part, giving way to smooth, well-rounded melodic constructions. We hear recollection-themes, with the shy flute melody standing out—a memory of spring, of short-termed happiness . . .

"The sunlit sky in spring—isn't it a cheat?" These are the first words we hear from Prince Andrei in the opera. In the Otradnoye village episode, new life with its irrepressible impulse towards happiness, its belief in the beautiful, overpowers the Prince's skeptical, searching soul. When he declares, "Spring, and love, and happiness, it's all but a stupid senseless cheat!"— the lovely vernal night theme, full of light and meaning, comes from the orchestra, as if refuting the hero's words, refusing to believe them. The joyful sense of renewal is rendered with a theme of such rare song-like beauty that there are few others like it, even in Prokofiev's work, so rich in melodic masterpieces.

Like Tolstoy, the composer sees Prince Andrei as one of the best representatives of Russian society, a patriot who dies courageously for his country. His speech on the Borodino field is full of pain and grief for the ravaged land of Russia, and of prophetic belief in victory.

The scene of Prince Andrei's encounter with Natasha in Mytishi and his death—an episode of the novel that Prokofiev instantly perceived as an opera scene—became the composer's masterpiece.

The monotonously rocking violin chords sound like a slow mournful lullaby. "Prince Andrei heard (he didn't know whether it was real, or just delirium) a low whispering voice, ceaselessly and measuredly repeating, 'Ipiti-piti-piti' and then, 'iti-ti' and again, 'ipiti-piti-piti' and again, 'iti-ti.' " Behind the stage, a women's chorus repeats, impassively and monotonously, the same drilling sound. Prince Andrei is delirious; a plaintive violin theme accompanies his words. The dying man thinks of the Motherland—"My country, Moscow's golden domes!"—and the theme of Kutuzov's aria sounds in the orchestra. A figure clad in white appears in the doorway and slowly approaches Prince Andrei: "It's you? What a pleasure!" The last consolation is his love that has gone through so many ordeals and comes back before he dies. "Love is life . . ." Prince Andrei utters. But the few lucid moments give way to heavy delirium. The sinister "piti-piti" comes again, as if numbering the last minutes of the dying man's life.

The second half of the opera is devoted to images of war. Foremost are the Russian people—the great force that crushed Napoleon's invasion—and wise general Kutuzov, a spokesman for the people's might and will.

The choral epigraph opens the opera with a powerful march of formidable dissonant chords: "The powers of two-and-ten tongues of Europe invaded Russia." Heroic melodies of folk-style

A. Frinberg as Pierre.

Scene from *War and Peace*: Prince
Andrei (Yuri Mazurok) and
General Kutuzov (Alexander
Vedernikov) before the battle of
Borodino.

O. Chishko as Pierre Bezukhov in
War and Peace.

construction symbolize the tremendous strength of the people. Like Tolstoy, Prokofiev emphasizes the idea of the heroes' indissoluble bond to the people. Those in the foreground enter the path of glory because, at a crucial moment, they act just like any ordinary soldier. "And, if I have to die . . . I'll do it no worse than others," Prince Andrei says proudly. Kutuzov's aria "O peerless people!" is full of boundless love for the people, of confidence in its might. The melody is majestic and song-like, like Russian folk songs; it serves as a characterization, both of the old wise general and of the heroic people.

Prokofiev had many doubts about scene 10. "A council?. . . And a military council, too? . . . In an opera?" And yet he succeeded in creating an expressive, dramatic scene, full of intense inner dynamics. The generals speak one after the other, trying painstakingly to decide the crucial question on which the fate of Russia depends: should Napoleon be fought as he approaches Moscow, or should the capital be surrendered, in order to preserve the army? Kutuzov's order to retreat from Moscow is the culmination of the scene. His words that express the will of the people are accompanied by the powerful, affirmative theme of the aria "O Peerless People!" As he is left alone, the old general is lost in deep, painful thought. As a confirmation of the wisdom of his decision, as a portent of future victory, the musical texture brightens up luminously, in major mode. The beautiful, inspired theme of his aria, which Prokofiev took from the music for the film *Ivan the Terrible*, is an exalted hymn to the great city. "Majestic, basked in sunlight, Mother of Russian cities, you lie before us, Moscow."

The scenes in Moscow occupied by the French are tragic. Fates of people from previously alienated class groups are intertwined: hatred for the enemy and resolution to fight unite everyone. Pierre, wearing a coachman's coat, roves around Moscow, determined to assassinate Napoleon. The courage of the Russians baffles even Napoleon: "What determination! They're Scythians!" The choral oath that concludes the scene is a stern call to fight.

In the final "Smolensky Road" scene, the heroic epic line is completed. The victorious people celebrate triumph over the enemy to the sounds of a powerful chorus based on Kutuzov's theme.

Absorbed in work on the opera, Prokofiev found time for other compositions as well. In Kazakhstan, he wrote the Flute Sonata and Piano Sonata No. 8. Acquaintance with fascinating Kazakh music gave him the idea of writing a merry opera based on folklore material. His attention was drawn by the amusing tale of a young Shah who had horns on his forehead. The Shah hides this from everyone, but he is secretly proud, regarding the horns as a mark of royalty. "I am going to write the opera by a new method, breaking the libretto into separate fragments, like shots in a film, and finding musical material to match each of those shots—such as I find most suitable for the given fragment," the composer explained. Larger plans took precedence over the opera which was never written, even though Prokofiev continued to think about it

Poster announcing the premiere of *War and Peace* in concert at the Grand Hall of the Moscow Conservatory.

for a long time.

The administration of the Leningrad S. M. Kirov Opera and Ballet Theatre invited Prokofiev to complete the ballet *Cinderella* and take part in the production. In June 1943, the indefatigable composer went to Perm, where the theatre had been evacuated. By the end of summer, he finished the piano-score of *Cinderella* (the production of the ballet had to be postponed) and a suite based on the material of *Semyon Kotko*. At the same time, Prokofiev created one of his brightest, finest works—the Flute Sonata. Even earlier, in France, the composer dreamed of writing a work for the flute, the instrument that he loved so much. The pictures of the composition—simple-hearted lyricism, smiling scherzo motifs, sometimes a humorous allusion to antique forms of music-making. It must have been inevitable that such a work should appear next to other, dramatic ones—the suite *1941*, *Ballad of a Boy*, *War and Peace*, Sonata No. 7. This islet of poetic lyricism is like a luminous dream, like a symbol of the happiness the fight was for.

That summer in Perm was rich in new impressions. The composer was enchanted by the natural environment in the ballet *Tale of the Stone Flower*.

From Perm, Prokofiev returned to Moscow and joined in the rehearsals of *War And Peace, Ballad of a Boy*. That autumn, he received another token of recognition of his art: Mikhail Ivanovich Kalinin awarded him the Order of Red Labor Banner in the Kremlin. Not long before that, the title of Honored Art Worker of the R.S.F.S.R. was bestowed on him.

The composer spent the summer of 1944, for the first time, in the Ivanovo Creative Work House of composers. The coming victory was a source of joyful excitement and renewed strength. It was during that summer, in Ivanovo, that D. Shostakovich's Trio for the memory of I. Sollertinsky and N. Myaskovsky's Cello Concerto were written. The joy of personal contact with colleagues, the beauty of nature—everything was favorable to work. With the usual iron discipline of his work habits, Prokofiev instituted an excellent custom at the Creative Work House: in the evening, everyone had to give his comrades an account of what he had done during the day. That summer, Prokofiev wrote such notable works as Piano Sonata No. 8 and Symphony No. 5.

Born in the years of the Great Patriotic War, the Symphony came as a proud hymn to courage, opening a world of light, harmony, victory over evil. The wide canvas of the symphony unfolds like a majestic epic narrative; its unhurried flow reminds one, at times, of the development of the heroic images in Borodin's symphonies, of the calm flow of Russian epic folk songs. The balance and proportion of forms, the harmony of sound links Symphony No. 5 to the classical tradition; the breadth of expression, the profoundly national character of the music bring it close to the epic *War and Peace*.

"In Symphony No. 5, I wanted to sing of free and happy man, of his mighty strength, his nobility, his spiritual purity. I can't

Prokofiev with Dmitry Kabalevsky (left) and Reinhold Glier at the composer's retreat in Ivanovo, 1945.

say I chose the theme: it was born in me and demanded to be expressed. I wrote the music that ripened in my soul and finally filled it."

Unhurriedly, as if conscious of its proud power, the main theme of the first movement of the symphony (Andante) unfolds. The melody flows, broad and free. At the same time, the intonations of Russian song are animated by the energy of dynamic rhythmic movement. The majestic solemnity of the main theme is set against the fine, delicate lyricism of the side theme. The circle of the principal pictures of movement 1 is closed by a sudden contrasting theme—playful and a little wary, like a character from a tale full of mystery. In the culminating conclusion of movement 1, the theme of the main voice is affirmed as a picture of courage triumphant.

The second movement of the cycle—the Allegro marcato—is one of Prokofiev's best symphonic Scherzos. The gracious, slightly angular theme seems to have fluttered out of Prokofiev's ballets. In the process of its development, a rich, many-sided image takes shape. The initial serenity gives way gradually to a mood of alarm and anxiety. The central episode, with its naive pastoral song and merry dance, is like a moving memory, after which the contrast of the recapitulation sounds even more ominous.

A lovely inspired melody forms the basis of the slow movement (Adagio). The orchestral texture is transparent and full-blooded at the same time, recalling the best of the mature Prokofiev's lyrical fragments: the pure, poetic lyricism of *Romeo and Juliet*, of *War and Peace*, of piano sonatas. Dramatic reality intrudes upon the unhurried narrative with the sorrowful sonorities of the middle part. It is a meditation full of grief, a wail for the ordeal of the people. The austere, well-proportioned forms of the structure are achieved by the smooth framing: after the middle episode, the carefree, serene lyricism of the initial theme reigns again.

Sergei Prokofiev receives his medal "For the defense of Moscow" from fellow composer Aram Khachaturian.

The exuberant finale (Allegro giocoso) completes the shapely symphonic form. The main theme of the first part of the symphony appears at the beginning of the finale, like a memory of the past. And then, like a glittering whirlwind, a dance theme bursts in, then a second, a third . . . Their generous variety creates a picture of an exuberant feast, a great joy of the people. The music glitters, shines with the bright colors of ringing piano strokes, with airy sparkling splashes of the harp. The sheen of gleaming sonorities grows brighter towards the conclusion—the highest point where joyful dance turns into a powerful triumph of heroism.

In Symphony No. 5, Prokofiev achieved not only the height of professional composing skill, but also great human and civic maturity. As in the other great works of those years—the symphonies of Shostakovich and Myaskovsky—features of a new hero of modern times were shaped in it.

The first performance of Symphony No. 5, on January 13, 1945, was an extraordinary one. The composer himself wielded the baton. "And, suddenly when Prokofiev stood at the stand and complete silence reigned," S. Richter recalls, "gun volleys boomed."

"His baton was raised already. He waited, and he didn't start until the cannons were silent. There was something very meaningful, very symbolic about that. It was a new frontier, common to everyone . . . and to Prokofiev, too . . .

"In Symphony No. 5, he rises in the full height of his genius. And, at the same time, the era, history, the war, patriotism, victory are all in that work . . . Victory of all—and Prokofiev's own victory. That was his final victory. He had always been victorious before, but here, as artist, he was victorious forever."

About the same time Symphony No. 5 was performed, came Piano Sonata No. 8. It completed the grandiose cycle of three sonatas—Nos. 6, 7, and 8—conceived before the war. In this triad, Prokofiev reveals his mastery of large-scale, monumental pianistic style. In the period of 1940-1944, they came, one after the other: the Sixth with its willful contrasts, the Seventh with its spirit of anxiety, and the Eighth—"the richest," S. Richter remarked. It was Richter who first performed Sonatas Nos. 6 and 7—a passionate champion of the composer's work, the author of remarkable memoirs about him, a pianist whom Prokofiev called the best "in the Soviet Union and on the whole round Earth." The Eighth was brilliantly executed by Emil Gilels late in 1944.

War left an indelible mark on the composer's soul and his art. He saw destruction, ruins, millions of victims. Prokofiev lost friends in the war (A. Afinogenov, V. Derzhanovsky, B. Demchinsky among them). From close friends—Vera Alpers, Asafiev who worked obsessively in the terrible conditions of siege and miraculously survived—he learned about the ordeals that the citizens of Leningrad had suffered. In his journeys all over the country, Prokofiev saw the mighty, heroic people struggle for victory over the enemy with the calm courage of the contemporaries of Alexander Nevsky going to battle against the Teutonic knights. The privations shared by everyone brought Prokofiev closer than ever to his people and his country. Many of those who observed him in the war years noticed changes in the composer's character: he became milder, simpler, friendlier. Heroic images of the people were beginning to prevail in his music. This reinforced the democratic quality of his style, made his art even more accessible and sociable.

Prokofiev met the days of victory, in spring 1945, at the Podlipki sanatorium near Moscow. Shortly after the memorable premiere of Symphony No. 5, a sudden attack of illness disabled him for a long time. From that time on, the composer would spend the rest of his life in a fierce fight with the disease. Accustomed to measure the value of each day he lived by the amount of work done, he was denied the opportunity to compose, and that bothered him most. As soon as he recovered a little, Prokofiev continued to work, despite doctors' warnings.

He wrote his first postwar works—the symphonic *Ode to the End of the War* and Symphony No. 6. The spirit of the *Ode* is best described by the epigraph to the finale: "Strike the bells, beat the tympani!" The grandiose sonorous power of the *Ode*,

Prokofiev with Evgeni Mravinsky after the premiere of Symphony no. 6 (Leningrad, October 11, 1947).

Natalia Dudinskaya as Cinderella,
Konstantin Sergeyev as the Prince.
"The principal thing I wanted to
render in the music of *Cinderella,*"
Prokofiev wrote shortly before the
premiere, "was the poetic love of
Cinderella and the Prince: the
birth and growth of the feeling, the
obstacles in its way, the realization
of the dream."

Galina Ulanova as Cinderella, V.
Rebuev as Father.

constructed as a one-part poem, is stunning. The festive exuberance of the *Ode* is an immediate, joyous response to the victory. In Symphony No. 6, it gives way to deep, intense thought. After the premiere of the Symphony in 1947, Prokofiev told Soviet music critic I. V. Nestiev, "Now, we all celebrate the victory that has been achieved, but each of us has unhealed wounds: one has lost his loved ones, another his health . . . One shouldn't forget that."

The Symphony's dramatic sharp contrasts and grim battlefield episodes were a reminder of the events of war. The majestic funeral procession (the central fragment of movement 1, Allegro moderato) is one of the most impressive pictures in the composition. Formidable pictures of war interrupt the serene, song-like flow of pensive melodies in movement 2 (Largo). They also intrude on the bright festive celebration in the finale, a note of anxious concern for the future . . .

Many works by Prokofiev premiered in 1945-1946. Theatres in the big cities worked with care and affection on productions of his operas and ballets. In Moscow, the Bolshoi Theatre produced *Cinderella* (R. Zakharov) and *Romeo and Juliet* (L. Lavrovsky); in Leningrad, the first eight scenes of *War and Peace* were performed at the MALEGOT (B. Pokrovsky), and S. M. Kirov Theatre produced *Cinderella* (K. Sergeiev) and *The Duenna* (I. Shlepyanov). Five new productions in a year—can there be greater testimony to the composer's wide popularity?

Evidence of the love of audiences for his music moved Prokofiev greatly. His close friends and family recalled how excited he would be about news of performances of his new works. A temporary improvement in his health allowed the composer to go to Leningrad, where the current season at the Leningrad Philharmonic was opened by the premiere of Symphony No. 6, conducted by E. Mravinsky. Sergei Sergeievich was as happy as ever to see the city of his youth. Symphony No. 6 was performed beautifully; theatre productions had talent and originality. Running successfully were *The Duenna, War and Peace* and also one of the most important works of those years—*Cinderella*.

The idea of a choreographic interpretation of the Cinderella story was conceived before the war. The composer discussed details of the future ballet with libretto writer Volkov and choreographer Chabukiani. A lover of amusing stage effects, he fantasized joyously, thinking of a ballet rich in exciting musical happenings. In the war years, while he was working on the epic *War and Peace*, the composer kept going back enthusiastically to the moving, unaffected tale of the kind little dowdy turned into a lovely princess. Numberless victims, the cruel war and all the suffering and blood could not make people forget the dream of beauty, of what they had left behind, in unforgettable peaceful life, and what they were fighting for. The music Prokofiev composed affirms the great power of sublime love, the triumph of good over evil. "The authors of the ballet wanted the spectator to see real people, people who feel and suffer, in this fairy-tale framing," Prokofiev wrote about *Cinderella*.

Cinderella has the best lyrical fragments in the ballet: the beau-

Olga Lepeshinskaya as Cinderella.

tiful, enchantingly sublime duets with the Prince; the famous Adagio in the ball scene; the lovely waltzes (S. Samosud used to call Prokofiev "King of Waltz"). The Waltz in the finale of Act I (Coda-Waltz in Act II), the Grand Waltz in Act II, the Slow Waltz in Act III reveal the beauty and power of the heroes' feelings. In them, we see Cinderella grown up suddenly. The Waltzes of Act II, full of passion—now subdued, now triumphantly exalted—are especially beautiful.

"In the music, Cinderella is characterized by three themes," Prokofiev wrote. "The first is Cinderella hurt; the second, Cinderella, dreamy and pure; the third general theme is Cinderella, happy and in love." Cinderella's themes outline the development of her character: from humility and helplessness to a joyful, proud awareness of the power of her love.

Prokofiev depicts with wit and invention the envious, vain world that surrounds Cinderella. Her malicious and stupid sisters are ridiculous. They quarrel all the time, practice gavotte dancing clumsily, fuss around awkwardly as they depart for the ball. Their characteristics are almost caricature-like. Rhythms are "dance-like," verging on primitivism, sometimes sharply angular; melodics are fractured, "affected," leaping; the orchestration sharp and grating.

For the first time, in *Cinderella*, Prokofiev had a chance to depict the fascinating world of mysterious magic and marvelous transformations. There are the picturesque portraits of the four fairies representing the four seasons. The scene of the clock striking at the ball, with tiny gnomes tapdancing to the fantastic sounds. One recalls the toy scherzo motives in *The Nutcracker*, the world of rhythmically ticking little clocks and clockwork miracles in the operas of Ravel—an artist for whom Prokofiev always felt a special love and closeness.

Prokofiev wrote about *Cinderella*: "I wanted this ballet to be as dance-like as possible. *Cinderella* is written in the tradition of old classical ballet. It has many variations, pas de deux, three waltzes, adagio, gavotte, mazurka." And, indeed, *Cinderella* is virtually saturated with dances, which, from an artistic point of view, proved to be very convincing in the fairy-tale ballet genre. The brilliant premieres in November 1945 in Moscow, and especially in the Kirov Theatre in Leningrad in April 1946, made the ballet an immediate, lasting success.

In 1947-1948 Prokofiev wrote his last opera—*The Story of a Real Man*. (The Russian word in the title implies that "Man" is used in the generic, not "masculine" sense.)

The war that had taken a toll of twenty million (Russian) lives was over. It revealed the question of the genuineness of spiritual values, the meaning of true Soviet patriotism; it showed examples of the mass heroism of the Soviet people. The story of Alexei Maresiev, told in 1946 by *Pravda's* war reporter Boris Polevoy, was the story of a simple Russian fellow who proved to all the world he could do what seemed to be the impossible.

The new opera was a work of remarkable wholeness and originality; the development of the plot is virtually centered

A scene from *Cinderella* at the Bolshoi Theater.

Prokofiev in the 1940s.

Evgeni Kibkalo as Alexei Maresiev
in *The Story of a Real Man*.

around the destiny of one hero. We see Alexei in the woods, in a guerrilla mud-hut, in the hospital. He goes through hours of physical training, goes to dancing parties to convince the doctors that he can fly. (Alexei Maresiev, a fighter pilot, survived a crash and spent two weeks living in the woods; Russian guerrillas saved his life, but both his legs had to be amputated. Maresiev got himself artificial legs and, despite doctors' protests, went back to flying.) And then, as a legitimate reward for the feat—back to the sky, on the first operational flight.

What Prokofiev really wanted to show was a strong Russian character, a heroic act in the process of formation. That is why the opera is almost devoid of distracting episodes and subplots. The composer rejected the alluring prospect of creating a full-range portrait of Alexei's beloved, Olga. Only the character of the Commissar, who courageously meets death face to face, plays an important role in the story. The old warrior seems to embody the people's heroism, the endurance and strength of all Russian heroes, the strength Alexei, too, discovers in himself. To emphasize this continuity, the national essence of heroic character, Prokofiev saturates the musical texture with Russian folk-song material.

Songs are introduced in the opera in the most dramatic episodes of the story. Alexei is delirious, tossing in bed after the major operation; he sees his mother, Olga, surgeons in white coats and weird masks. Nurse Klavdia, sitting near him, sings "The Green Grove." The pensive, unhurried melody is comforting and lulling; it chases the painful visions away. Klavdia sings her second song at a tragic moment, after the death of the Commissar, hero of the Civil War who provided moral support for all the wounded. "O my sweet and fleeting dream," Klavdia sings in a low voice, and her song expresses the subdued pain of loss, the light sorrow of memories. The song of the collective farmers, "A Young Oak Grew in Plavni," which we first hear when Alexei, half dead, is found in the forest, embodies the great power of the people.

Prokofiev at work.

During the Great Patriotic War, Prokofiev wrote lyrical songs, "The Soldier's Sweetheart" and "A Warrior's Love." In the opera, he used them to create the character of Alexei's selfless, devoted fiancee Olga. The merry popular song "Anyuta," the humorous duet "Well, every man must marry," are little islets of happiness in the intense, dramatic story.

The originality of the music in *The Story of a Real Man,* its simple, song-like language, the burning actuality of its problematic contents were fully appreciated by audiences—but not until 1960, when the opera about human valor was heard from the stage of the U.S.S.R. Bolshoi Theatre. Twelve years earlier, the opera had been received very differently. The musicians who gathered at the Kirov Theatre for a closed hearing failed to understand the novelty and charm of the new work. The response to Prokofiev's music at that time was mixed.

The poor performance must have influenced this reaction, too; the production had been prepared in a hurry. Prokofiev took the failure with his usual courage and self-confidence, looking forward to new works. On the day of the ill-fated hearing, D. B.

Kabalevsky dropped in to see Prokofiev, who was staying at the "Astoria" hotel. He found the composer seated at his desk. Sergei Sergeievich greeted Kabalevsky with the words, "Look, this is the theme of the Lady." His imagination was already possessed by the idea of the new ballet, *Tale of the Stone Flower.*

The composer had a wonderful literary source—Pyotr Petrovich Bazhov's collection *The Mountain-green Casket.* (Note: "Mountain-green" is the semi-precious stone, malachite). The tales, written in the manner of Urals "mystery tales," wise and realistically earthy, full of sublime poetic beauty and colorful fantasy, became a true poetic revelation for Prokofiev, who was in love with the nature of the Urals. "You know," Sergei Sergeievich told choreographer L. Lavrovsky, "the theme of the Lady of the copper Mountain will begin to torment me soon; I don't know yet what it will be like, but it will torment me soon."

And now, it was written—the beautiful theme that opens the ballet. The brilliant sounds of trumpets emphasize its power; the breadth and the willful freedom of their intonations speak not only of proud beauty and imperious authority, but also of generosity, capacity for forgiveness and sacrifice . . .

The leading characters of the ballet—craftsman Danila, his faithful fiancee Katerina—seem to have emerged from the crowd of common folk. Their story is set against the background of colorful, graphic mass scenes. The large dance suite adorns the scene of Katerina's engagement to Danila, in the second scene of Act I. The maidens' dance, gracious and delicate, is followed by Danila's, dynamic and dashing, and then by the perky "Bachelors' Dance." Brutal Severyan appears, and the music changes abruptly. Frightening sonorities, sharp and harsh intonations characterize the "killer" supervisor. Danila is inflamed with the desire to find the secret of the beautiful stone flower which the Lady of the Copper Mountain keeps in her underground kingdom. "Beauty is revealed in that flower"—and Danila goes away to seek the miracle.

In Act II, we see the Lady of the Copper Mountain and her realm. "High trees stand there, but not such as in our woods; they're trees of stone. Some of marble, some of mountain-green. And the grass below is of stone, too. Blue, red, of all colors . . . The sun is nowhere to be seen and yet the light is as bright as just before sunset . . . Big bells of mountain-green hang from the shrubs, a little stibium star in each. Fiery bees sparkle over those flowers, and the starlets tinkle ever so thinly, like a song." The Lady tempts Danila with her charms and her glittering riches. The arrogant meandering breaks of her theme are especially refined in those episodes. Danila is firm in his loyalty to Katerina and his determination to find the stone flower.

Prokofiev called Scene 6 "the Urals Rhapsody." Action takes place at a fair. One dance follows after another. Exuberant merriment, perky energetic rhythms give way to the flowing lyricism of the girls' round dance. Severyan's appearance at the fair is sinister, frightening. The drunk, violent supervisor makes advances to Katerina; but the magic of the Lady of the Copper

A scene from *The Stone Flower:* Galina Ulanova as Katerina, Vladimir Preobrazhensky as Danila.

**Prokofiev at the opening of the
First All-Union Composers'
Congress in Moscow, on April 19,
1948.**

N. Chkalova as Katerina and Maya Plisetskaya as the Lady of the Copper Mountain in *The Stone Flower*.

Mountain turns him into stone. In the last scene of the ballet, Katerina fights the Lady herself for Danila. The imperious, resolute themes of the underground queen clash with Katerina's lyrical melodies, which now become firm and assertive.

In no other work did Prokofiev so powerfully express the theme of Nature's beauty and might. His last ballet is a hymn to the Russian land and its great riches, to the greatness of man, the craftsman who values those treasures, preserves them and gives them to his fellow men.

In the postwar years, preservation of peace became a chief task of all progressive humanity. In the name of peace, the first World Festivals of democratic youth and students were held in Prague and Budapest. Writers, artists, composers created inspired works on this great subject. Prokofiev's monumental oratorio, *On Guard of Peace*, a setting of poetry by S. Marshak, was one of the most outstanding works of that time. "Poet Samuil Marshak and I worked on this oratorio with one overwhelming feeling: to make a contribution to the noble cause of peace," Prokofiev said.

"Scarcely has the Earth recovered from the storms of war"—thus, with an exalted phrase of the chorus and the narrator's intense recitation, starts the oratorio. The first four numbers tell of the ordeals of wartime, of the heroes who fought for their country. The oratorio's most poetic, climactic fragments are the central numbers devoted to children. "Lullaby," with its beautiful flowing melody, gained great popularity. The "We Do Not Need a War" fragment, for which Marshak wrote the lyrics later, during the rehearsals, became the best part of the oratorio.

> In the vast and cozy class
> It is silent in the morning.
> The schoolboys and schoolgirls are busy:
> They are writing, with white on black
> They are writing, with black on white
> Writing with chalk and pen:
> "We do not need a war!"

Prokofiev was excited and worried before the premiere. The first recital, on December 19, 1950 in the Column Hall of the House of Unions (the radio premiere had been broadcast earlier) was a great success. The warm approval the new composition met from the workers of a Moscow plant cheered the ailing composer. His music was understood and needed, and that was the chief purpose of his work.

The last stage of Prokofiev's life was a hard one. He often suffered acute, heavy attacks of hypertonia. From 1949 on, the composer led the life of an ascetic. He scarcely left his country house at Nikolina Mountain. Attendance at concerts became rare; he had to see *Cinderella* at the Bolshoi Theatre one act at a time. He could not move, talk or read too much. Yet no sacrifice made to the disease distressed the composer as much as the restrictions on his work.

The explanation for the amazing productivity of his last years is that the creative process was going on all the time, never interrupted. Those who knew the composer remember his remarkable

Prokofiev in the country. "With his full, sensitive, passionate receptivity to nature, he did not 'enjoy' it but, in a way, became one with it." *(Myra Mendelson-Prokofieva)*

ability to think about music in any circumstances, no matter what he was doing. He could play chess, walk in the woods, talk, listen to readings from his favorite books—and go on composing in his mind. The musical ideas he had at those moments were written down on any shred of paper he had near at hand—notes of the chess game, a newspaper, a cigarette pack. In the last years of his life, this method of work prevailed: the daily work norm prescribed by doctors was gradually reduced to less and less. "Can't they understand it's easier for me to write down a melody than to keep it in my head?" In the rare minutes he was allowed to work, he hurried feverishly to do as much as he could. Myra Alexandrovna recalls that he worked on seven compositions simultaneously in the final months.

Despite the disease and the strict regime, he was never idle. In the late 30s, Sergei Sergeievich said, "I don't like being—I like doing." That was how he remained in the final years, preserving the rare gift of enjoying life, seeing its beauty, being a part of it. He was delighted by the nature of the suburbs of Moscow and took great pleasure in gardening: "My father was an agriculturist, after all." Radio and records were very important in the composer's life. Myra Alexandrovna read aloud to him. Chekhov, Pushkin, Tolstoy, Gorky were his favorites.

Prokofiev often met with musicians. Among them were S. Richter, to whom Piano Sonata No. 9 is dedicated, D. Kabalevsky, S. Samosud, N. Golovanov, choreographer L. Lavrovsky. In those years, he worked on Symphony No. 7, Symphony-Concerto for Cello with orchestra, Cello Sonata, *Pushkin Waltzes* for symphony orchestra, revisions of Piano Sonata No. 5 and other early compositions.

Of all the creative achievements of Prokofiev's final years, Symphony No. 7, first performed in 1952, is probably the brightest, the most sublime and harmonious. Prokofiev's last symphony won him the title of Lenin prize laureate. But that was five years after the premiere, when the composer was no longer alive.

The composer's dream of sublime and beautiful simplicity is realized in the symphony with rare artistic perfection. The modest four-movement cycle presents a string of various pictures, all pictures of light and good. The opening of the symphony is marvelous; with a prolonged bass note in the background, the first violins start a lyrical melody of Russian folk music quality. The music of movement 2, with its engaging sudden humorous contrasts and turns, is inspired and poetic. The short, song-like third movement leads to the finale; the music seems to fly forth, full of youthful exaltation and energy. The joy, the dynamics, even the passion of the pictures of the finale give way, in the very end, to the tender lyricism of a theme from movement 1. The magical, disappearing sonorities, mellow colors fading away—it is like a quiet exit, a farewell . . .

The composer could not attend the performance of the symphony. On the following day, friends came to his house at Nikolina Mountain to tell him about it. D. B. Kabalevsky re-

The manuscript of Symphony no. 7.

Prokofiev's house on the Nikolina Mountain.

The last photograph of Prokofiev (1952).

called, "Sergei Sergeievich was not feeling well and was in bed. He smiled so happily, he looked so animated when we told him about the success. He asked us about it over and over again, as if he suspected we just wanted to cheer him up and give his energy a boost." Prokofiev had the joyful experience of witnessing the success of the symphony at the first recital, on October 11, 1952. The new work, performed by the All-Union Radio Orchestra and conducted by Samosud, was received enthusiastically.

Throughout the winter, Prokofiev worked intensely. Among his new plans were Piano Sonata No. 10 (he had time to write only the first two pages) and Sonata No. 11, op. 138. On March 1, 1953 rehearsals of *Tale of the Stone Flower* started at the Bolshoi. The premiere Sergei Sergeievich was so eager to see was in preparation. Full of projects, longing passionately for creative work, the composer worked on necessary alterations in the ballet. On March 5, he submitted the full score of the duet of Katerina and Danila and had it delivered to the theatre. That was the last day of his life.

In March 1953, a most outstanding musical genius died in Moscow. Prokofiev's work is as original, rich and multi-sided as the era from which he emerged. The greatest men and women of art crossed the composer's path. Life brought him together with artists of different countries, times, worlds. Taneyev, Rimsky-Korsakov, Glazunov were among his teachers. Richter, Ulanova, Shostakovich were among those who had creative contact with him toward the end of his life.

At the start of the century, the recent conservatory student with a brash manner pioneered in Russian art. Over the thundering avalanche of passages in piano concertos, over the deafeningly triumphant orchestra sounds, came a passionate young voice. A voice that sneered at the old-fashioned, the trite, the mediocre, that called for destruction for the sake of creation, confident in the beauty of tomorrow. Prokofiev could be tender and pathetic, and his laughter was not always happy. "A classical composer is a madman who composes things his generation can't understand." This paradoxical statement is a natural and legitimate one when it comes from him. He was always ahead. Not only the contents of his work, but even the language he spoke was new. An inexhaustible inventor and visionary, he was always inventing when he was creating—new methods of writing (his stubborn, assertive handwriting and his writing without vowels are quite characteristic!), stage effects, the gestures of his heroes and, of course, a unique musical language.

"When a composer says he has found his language at last and from now on he will speak it, that is the moment when he begins to regress." Prokofiev's life is an example of never-ending quest, tireless work, readiness for bold experiment. Each of his works is a new step forward. "A composer must always seek new means of expression. Each work must have a technique of its own. Otherwise, he will repeat himself; and that, inevitably, is the beginning of the end."

The composer's uniqueness and originality were never lost in

Manuscript of Sonata no. 9 with the dedication to Svyatoslav Richter.

the abundance of the unforgettable encounters life granted him so generously, or in his long travels all over the world. "Prokofiev's music can always be recognized and distinguished from any other music . . . It is sharp, astringent, intensively dynamic, valiantly impulsive . . .It is a music of movement, a music of healthy life that knows no exhaustion," B. Asafiev wrote in 1927. It was not only in his youth that Prokofiev stirred amazement. Toward the end of his life, each of his works was a surprise—whether it was the peaceful tenderness of Symphony No. 7 or the intimate simplicity of Sonata No. 9. The composer's last works are brightened by his kind smile, a smile full of the mellow light of wisdom.

Throughout his life, Prokofiev was a national artist, a bard of his country. Epic majesty and warm quiet lyricism, the generosity of melodies saturated with folk-song intonations, the fineness of polyphonic writing reminiscent of traditional Russian part-singing with subsidiary voices—such are the characteristic qualities of his artistic style.

Prokofiev's "great, willful talent" (Lyadov) remained, in its ceaseless renewal, flesh of the flesh of Russian classical tradition. The graphic accuracy and psychological depth were inherited from Dargomyzhsky and Mussorgsky. The powerful scope of his music is reminiscent of Borodin. The captivating, sublime waltzes, with a shade of nostalgia now and then in their noble refinement, bring to mind the lyricism of Glinka, Tchaikovsky, Glazunov. And the picturesque fantasy, now ominously sinister, now toy-like, scherzo-ish, is linked to the achievements of Glinka, Rimsky-Korsakov, Lyadov.

His music unites in a quaint but unassailably logical way the most contradictory distinctive qualities of the times, loyalty to the humanistic traditions of Russian and foreign art and bold breakthroughs into the future. "Prokofiev never was a captive of experiment or a slave of academicism," American composer R. Harris remarked. High artistic sensitivity, the special spiritual refinement of an offspring of the Russian school of music led Prokofiev to create an artistic style unique in the motley variety of 20th century cultural life. Its distinctive features—harmony, proportion, beauty—resurrect the harmonious perfection of classical art.

He succeeded in reproducing the reality of his time, the light and darkness of today's world, even when writing of antiquity. The new world he created in his art is not only a world of dynamic rhythms, thundering steel, energy and power, but also a world of infinite love of man, man who is great in all times, capable of courage, self-sacrifice and highest feeling. Prokofiev's imperiously commanding music calls for peace and goodness. The restless human spirit will turn, ever and ever again, to his works, filled with a voice of life and love.

His luminous genius was born of the twentieth century. And, the more time passes since the day of his sudden death, the more one sees how much people need the art of Sergei Prokofiev, an art of courage and humanity.

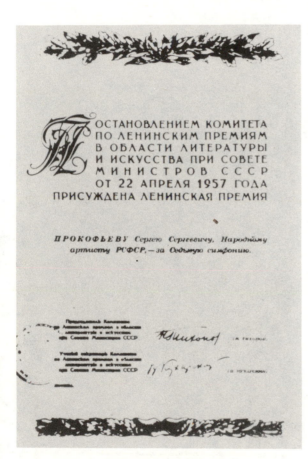

The Lenin prize diploma, awarded to Prokofiev posthumously (in 1957) for his Symphony no. 7.

The opening scene of *War and Peace* at the Bolshoi Theater.